BERT BISSELL R___

*To Mayor, Cllr. Wilson.
From, Vicar Street Men's Bible Class.
September 8th, 2002.*

An anthology of tributes and stories

**Compiled by David Monkton
and Alan J. Wedge**

© David Monkton & Alan Wedge, 2001

All rights reserved.
No part of this publication may be reproduced stored in a retrieval system or transmitted in any form or by any means; electronic, mechanical, photocopying, recording or otherwise, without the prior, express permission of the publishers and authors in writing.

ISBN 0 9534295 2 0
Softback, 80 pages. 210x148mm.
Typeset Dutch 801 Roman 10/11/18.

Cover illustration: From a painting 'Primitive Methodists' by W.H.Y. Titcomb by courtesy of Dudley Archives. Overlaid is a badge of the Vicar Street Young Men's Bible Class.

Published by
Fairway Folio
Christian Publishing Services
Alsager, Cheshire 01270 874662

Printed by
J. H. Brookes (Printers) Ltd.
Lower Bryan Street, Hanley, Stoke-on-Trent ST1 5AX

Contents

Foreword	4
Bert Bissell Remembered	6
What 'The Recorder' Said	8
Earlier memories	12
First impressions	21
Dudley's 'First' Probation Officer	27
Cameos	31
Ben Nevis, and the Cause of Peace	41
Some general tributes to him	50
Things never forgotten	59
Tributes from other Class members - past and present	63
Summing up The Journey	71
'We are watchers of a beacon...'	75
Bibliography	77
List of contributors	78

Foreword

It is an honour and a pleasure to write the preface to a book prepared as a tribute to Bert Bissell. Bert Bissell was a great Methodist layman. Methodists in the Midlands, in the British Isles and indeed Methodists throughout the world can be proud of him: this was recognised when Bert Bissell was presented with the World Methodist Award for Peace. In honouring this lay Methodist, we honour the ministry of lay people.

Bert Bissell also supported the call to Presbyteral ministry of twenty members of his young men's Bible class in Vicar Street, Dudley. He worked professionally as a Probation Officer. As a layman he worked with people of all faiths, all skin colours, all church denominations, across international boundaries, and related prayer to political affairs seeking a society that is just and fair for all.

Bert Bissell's pride and joy was the Bible class. It was always well attended. A liturgy of four hearty hymns, Bible reading, and an Address. What was the secret of its success? Bert Bissell's style and key to his success was utter respect for people of all ages, all faiths, all skin colours. He had the ability to give time, attention and a listening ear to each person. More than this he helped people to relate faith to daily life, and to find excitement in sport and mountain climbing. His style and example is needed today more than ever, and particularly in the context of the current furore over race, racism and racists. It says that racism and racist attitudes, words and attacks have to be made utterly disrespectful and are to be challenged.

Bert Bissell rooted all his activities in a life of prayer and the teachings and example of the great 'young man from Nazareth, Jesus Christ'.

Bert Bissell provides a model for us. This book will inspire many.

The Revd. Inderjit S. Bhogal
President of the Methodist Conference, 2001

Bert Bissell Remembered

This is not a biography, or history of his life: that has already been meticulously and carefully portrayed in the book God's Mountaineer by the late Don Bissell and Barry Weetman[1]. It is a compilation of tributes to Bert at the time of his death and responses to an appeal placed in the Express and Star and Methodist Recorder for stories and incidents about him.

At the funeral service at Vicar Street, Dudley, the Revd. Geoffrey Bruce (the then Superintendent Minister of the Dudley and Netherton Circuit) said.

> 'A small group recently met to prepare a service for 'All Saint's Day,' and in the course of our conversation I asked the others for the names of anyone they considered to be a present-day saint of their acquaintance. The first name mentioned was Bert Bissell.
>
> The other day I came across a list of the four qualities which the Roman Catholic Church looks for in those she canonizes as saints. "Loyalty to the faith, heroism in time of testing, the power to do what ordinarily would seem humanly impossible, and radiance amid the storm strains of life." All these qualities were found in Bert.'

Chris Hughes Smith recalls how he heard the same thought expressed at the Diamond Jubilee Rally of The Class in Dudley Town Hall. when he was invited to speak as the incoming President of the Methodist Conference in 1985.

> 'The invitation came in a typewritten letter that filled the page, and was couched in terms that could not be refused. The occasion was memorable. Members of the Bible Class, older and younger, turned out in strength; The Gentlemen Songsters sang. The Chairman, Derek Vonberg was in his place, and the Mayor of Dudley brought the town's greetings. She, Dr Kate Rogers, was to the point. "You know about Saints, don't you," she told the congregation, "St Francis of Assisi, Mahatma Ghandi, Mother Teresa, and such like. Now what I want to say is that we have got a Saint in Dudley. It's Bert Bissell, the leader of this Bible Class."'

Bert was a remarkable person. You could say of him 'once seen, never forgotten.' He was a very different person from Mother Teresa, but, like her, he certainly had 'singleness of mind,' and an amazing variety of people have been influenced by his life.

We have tried to group themes and anecdotes together, and editorial amendments have been kept to a minimum. This has not been an easy task.

There are over sixty contributors to this anthology who all speak in their own unique way, and even now there are fresh stories and incidents coming to light. There may appear to be some repetition of themes but even when this happens, some fresh glint of Bert's distinctness comes out in the process.

We would like to say a big thank you to all the people who have contributed to this publication, and to the Church Council of Vicar Street Methodist Church who have covered the financial outlay involved to publish this anthology.

We have not been able to recognise all the people who are in the photographs; but if readers will let us know who they are, it would be helpful to have a record, and, if possible, inform them that they are on the photographs used.

David Monkton
Alan Wedge

What 'The Recorder' Said

We felt it appropriate to begin with one of the most widely read tributes to him.

Alan Davies, one of the senior ministerial members of the class, together with additional information from journalist Barry Weetman - a great supporter of Bert's work over many years - wrote this tribute for the Methodist Recorder. Barry is a journalist for the Methodist Recorder. He also undertook the task of editing the book 'God's Mountaineer' after the untimely death of Donald Bissell, one of Bert's Nephews.

Many of the themes touched on this particular chapter will be expanded by a wide spectrum of individuals in their contributions to this book.

'My future' wrote Alan, 'was settled one stormy day in 1942 when a Dudley Corporation carpenter and the town's probation officer took shelter in the same doorway. For some reason or other the carpenter mentioned that his nephew played the piano; the probation officer wanted someone to play the harmonium at his Friday evening prayer group meeting; and so began the contact with Bert Bissell which changed my life.

Scores of others could write similar stories of this extraordinary man.

First and foremost Bert Bissell was a 'head-hunter' for his Lord. If he saw someone with a particular gift or talent he did his level best through friendship and encouragement to bring that person into the service of Christ. I know from my own life how much time and trouble Bert took with me. On foot, by bicycle or in later years conveyed in friends' cars, Bert was always out and about, visiting, inviting or persuading.

What was Bert's secret? It was certainly not political correctness. Bert's was a totally male world, not because of any antipathy to the opposite sex but because he saw ministry to them as the province of other people. Nor was it through what we now call charisma. He was plain in speech, dress and appearance, his accent a mixture of Coventry and Black Country which inspired countless imitations by his young men behind his back. Part of the reason for his impact was the way he could convince the person he was with that they were special folk doing a wonderful job, whether it was road-sweeping or being a hospital consultant. In another man this approach might be dismissed as mere flattery but with Bert it was an uncanny knack of making people aware of their own worth and the unique contribution that they could make.

Allied to this was Bert's ability to get alongside people of all faiths and of no faith, of every ethnic group and of every social class. In Dudley and Fort William you will find countless men and women who looked on Bert as a friend who otherwise would seem to have nothing in common.

Although a life-long Methodist and a convinced evangelical, Bert had friends in every part of the Christian family, among the Sikh community and among the Shinto faith in Japan. All this was never at the expense of hiding or blurring his own faith but was brought about by the way he treated others with respect and consideration.

Bert lived so much for others that despite his high public profile in later years it was not easy to see the private person. For instance for all my friendship for more than fifty years I never knew how Bert voted in elections, nor did I know much about his family and early life until Don Bissell wrote his biography. Perhaps it was his love of the hills in general and Ben Nevis in particular when Bert could best be seen as himself. He climbed most of the highest in Britain scores of times.

The Vicar Street Bible Class first went to the summit of the Ben in 1937. Both Bert and members of the class visited Fort William and Ben Nevis every year since. Needless to say, even Bert's love of the hills was related to his faith and work.

Just as Jesus took his disciples, so Bert took his young men into the mountains for their spiritual growth and to deepen the bonds of fellowship. By today's standards there was an amazing innocence, and lack of awareness of danger in those early expeditions. I recall one Easter Monday on the Snowdon Horseshoe the look of incredulity on the faces of 'proper' climbers on seeing one member of the Vicar Street path in wellington boots and carrying an umbrella. And back in 1944 eight of us were almost benighted on Beinn a Ghlo in Perthshire and were fortunate enough to find shelter in a stalker's cottage. (This incident is recorded in detail by Ron Towe.) In later years Bert was well aware both of the risks and public reaction if accidents occurred and so began his long association with the Lochaber Mountain Rescue team who accompanied us on all our later Ben Nevis climbs.

After 1945 the Peace Cairn on Ben Nevis represented so many of the issues he held dear and each of his 107 climbs of the Ben was a spiritual pilgrimage, as it was for literally hundreds of people who climbed with him over the years. And when he was finally unable physically to make the climb, as on the 50th anniversary of the building of the cairn, Bert watched from Achintee and was with us in spirit every step of the way.

It was VJ Day 1945 when the peace campaigns of the Vicar Street Class and Bert first gained momentum. They were visiting Fort William and Bert took boys from the class to the top of the Ben where they created what was to become the beginnings of an international peace cairn. There began a vision of prayerful and practical peace campaigning which led to Bert becoming a regular and welcome visitor to the Russian, American and Japanese embassies in London. He and the class called on the Russians and Americans to broadcast messages of peace and goodwill from space. The Americans did just that at

Christmas 1968.

Bert Bissell's friendliness towards the Japanese aroused severe criticism from some quarters because of atrocities towards Allied servicemen during the Second World War. However a lasting relationship was formed between the Bible Class and the atomic-ravished city of Hiroshima which spread to include the borough of Dudley, Coventry Cathedral and what was the Lochaber District centred on Fort William.

In 1962, Dudley class members felt called by God to invite Japanese friends to place a tablet on the cairn alongside others from all over the world.

Eventually, after six years of letter writing and visits to the Japanese Embassy, a black granite tablet was received from Hiroshima. Both Dudley and Fort William responded by sending tablets for display in the Peace Park at Hiroshima which is marked by an official twinning. As a response to his peace efforts and ties with Hiroshima Bert Bissell visited Japan for 16 days in 1978 as a guest of the Japanese government.

With a few years of leading peace climbs in Ireland, north and south, Bert went to South Africa as a roving peace ambassador in 1992 and spoke at a rally beside Table Mountain. On his return he reported: "I have seen the first glow of the morning of deliverance and freedom." There have since been exchange visits between South African and Dudley teachers arising from the strong relationship he maintained with Dudley schools.

Bert Bissell received the MBE in 1959. He received the freedom of the borough of Dudley in 1981 and the freedom of Lochaber 10 years later. In June 1987, he received the World Methodist Peace Award jointly with an American Federal judge. He recorded his 100th climb on Ben Nevis in 1988 and the following year received from Fort William Rotary Club the world Rotary International medal.

At the end of the day I suspect that the full Bert Bissell is to be found in the detailed diaries kept throughout his life. Bible class members have been known to check queries about their own past history by asking Bert to look back at the diary of a particular year. For his writing up the diary and prayer went together and many of us have cause to be grateful for the knowledge that he prayed for us day by day.

The last conversation I had with Bert was typical of the man. In recent years his deafness meant he often had to guess what people were saying to him, which led to some surreal situations. Our phone call ended with Bert saying he had great plans for what should happen on Ben Nevis in two years' time. When I put the phone down I said to my wife, less than graciously, "What's he on about now?" She reminded me Bert was referring to the millennium.

Even at 96 years of age he held to the Bible class motto, "The best is yet to be" and was working out how best to use the celebrations for the furtherance of the Kingdom. I suspect most of us who knew him expected him to be around for the millennium and to be taken by helicopter to the top of Ben Nevis on his

100th birthday. For those of us influenced by him, Glen Nevis will not only be arguably one of the most beautiful places on God's earth, but it will also be Bert's Glen.'

Earlier memories

Earlier memories start with the formative years in Bert's life, the development of Class at Vicar Street, the war years, and his great love of climbing – which led to so much more. The first contribution comes from the representative from Bablake School in Coventry.

Coventry Days

Contribution by Terry Proctor - Master at Bablake School, Coventry - at the Memorial Service held at the Town Hall, Dudley on Sunday 10th January 1999.

'Bert came to Coventry in 1915 when his father took up a ministerial appointment. Enquiries were made about schools, and Bert took the entrance exam, won a scholarship, and started at Bablake School, a school which then had 350 pupils, and had been founded in 1344.

Bert was then 13, coming to the school at a later age than most, but he discovered that his considerable sporting talents helped to win him rapid acceptance. One of the first things he was asked was, "Can you play football?" He could - very well - and he was in the first team almost immediately, later captaining the team.

He wasn't quite so successful on the musical side. The music master played some notes and asked Bert to say what they were. He replied "I haven't the faintest idea." The master said "You're no good for the choir." Bert was very pleased about this as it meant he didn't have to go to the practices.

Bert gained a second scholarship as a boarding pupil for 2 years and became one of the 36 boarders, or Indoor Boys, as they were called. One day the Matron sent out for 2lbs of fish for the 36 boys - they called it Matron's Miracle the way it went round. Another time when the indoor boys beat the school soccer team the Matron gave them a pot of jam - between the 36 of them. Bert became the residential Head Prefect and one of his responsibilities was for the fire drill. He decided the 'fire' should be in Matron's room. He therefore went barging in there and answered her startled, "Whatever's the matter?" with a calm, "Oh, it's alright Matron - just a fire!"

Bert was a talented cricketer, captaining the cricket team from a young age. A highlight of each year for Bert was when Bablake played Rugby School at cricket. The whole school had a half-day off and went on the train to Rugby to support the team. In the School versus Staff match, Bert was delighted when they got the Headmaster out for one.

Bert was the only member of the school cricket team who was a boarder and he had to organise the indoor boys for a cricket match against the school team. He had the indoor boys out training at six in the morning and they beat the school team. Bert had cricket trials with Warwickshire County Cricket Club and the Public Schools XI.

He was in the Debating Society and got his first training in public speaking. He always felt indebted to Bablake for the opportunities to develop his leadership qualities.

Being Head Prefect Indoors, lads came with their troubles and Bert would help. Looking back Bert said this helped him with his work with young people and his work as a probation officer.

As captain of the soccer and cricket teams he had to go onto the stage every Monday morning to tell the school how the 1st XI got on, on the Saturday.

As Head Prefect Indoors, Bert had the honour of hoisting the Union Flag on the school tower for the Armistice on 11th November 1918. Bert was a victim of the flu that swept across Europe, had spells off school and eventually had to leave school because of illness.

He started selling clothing and footwear and always felt grateful to the Headmaster, other masters and Bablake parents who gave him the orders that set him up.

Bert came regularly to our school concerts and prize-givings, and had been guest speaker at the latter event. At the end of each item in a concert you were left in no doubt of what Bert thought of it as a loud, "Marvellous," could be heard throughout the hall. After the concerts and prize-givings I would sometimes take Bert home and the cakes would come out and I would be treated

'Climbing Snowdon in the mid 1940's - a popular outing for Easter Mondays. (Bert wearing trilby.)

to a midnight feast. I have come to the conclusion that everyone over seventy-five lives on little cakes with pink or yellow icing.

Bert was very generous in so many ways. He sent money every year for scripture prizes to be presented at prize-giving and he enjoyed meeting the prize winners.

He presented a trophy to be given to the form which had made a significant contribution to charity.

I took groups of Bablake pupils up Ben Nevis with him on three occasions including the 1988 climb when the television programme "Bert and the Ben," was made. I had no video recorder up to then, so had to go and buy one so I could record the programme. Bert kept in touch with those pupils for years afterwards, visiting some in Coventry for tea and sending Christmas cards.

So Bert's links with Coventry are not confined to the football club. He has given slide shows at the Methodist Church in Coventry that I attend and hundreds of Bablake School pupils are going to miss him. We have one word for him: "*Marvellous*.'"

TP

Earlier friendships and experiences

> *Ron Towe first met Bert in 1939 through the 'League of Youth,' the club Bert ran for lads from the Intermediate School.*

'We met at the Temperance Hall,' he writes, 'and speakers were footballers, cricketers, boxers etc. This was Bert's feeder club from our school from which he hoped members would join the 'Young Men's Class.' Many of us did.

During the next six years I was deeply involved with Bert and Vicar Street Church. They were years which gave me 'foundation for life' and Bert was my friend for 60 years.

We walked to Worcester: we walked to Birmingham to hear the President of the Methodist Conference, Leslie Weatherhead; we climbed in Wales, the Lake District and Scotland. One day I met Bert on his way home from court where he told me he had stood bail of £50 for a lad. " I hope he doesn't let me down," he said. " I haven't got £50!"

On another occasion I accompanied him to a preaching appointment in Bilston. He told me there were never more than a handful of old people in the congregation who did very little to encourage others to swell the numbers. " I am taking as the text for my sermon 'Why sit we here till we die?'" he said.

I holidayed with Bert and Class at Keswick in 1941, Killin, Perthshire in 1942 and 1943 and Pitlochry in 1944. After a week with us he would take a well- earned holiday on his own at places like Portree, Isle of Skye, and Fort William. It was in the next year, 1945 that the class first went to Fort William. Peace was declared, the Cairn was built and history was made.

My time at Vicar Street was through the dark days of war and very traumatic times. I sometimes did fire watching with Bert, sleeping in the small room at the back of the old chapel.

In November 1940 Bert took a small party of us to Coventry on the weekend following the blitz. The devastation was unbelievable. Bert was heartbroken. We visited Bert's eldest brother Sidney who lived on the outskirts. I wondered on the bus journey if we would ever pass along a road with no buildings bombed.

On holiday in Killin

The photograph which I enclose, has on it Ernie Price (see Killin Group photograph above) – the only Class member to die on active service, Harry Davies, Jack Lee, myself, Harry Oliver, Robin Bratt – my best friend who became a 'Bevin Boy', then a Methodist Minister and at an early age was tragically killed in a hit and run road accident. Sidney Marsh, Ray Turner, and Cyril Waller (seated on ground). Harry Oliver, Ernie and Sid were great friends – all ex Intermediate School and were awaiting 'call up' when this photograph was taken.

Beinn a Ghlo (The Mountain of Mist)

In 1944, we holidayed in Pitlochry. The highlight of this holiday was the climbing of Beinn a Ghlo – 3671 feet high. We took the train to Blair Atholl, began the climb and were soon in thick mist. We climbed for several hours, the mist never relented and then we were on a ridge walking along a level spur. Suddenly the mist cleared momentarily. Across the valley was another spur with a herd of deer on the horizon. Bert said we should have been on that spur.

Down came the mist again. We retraced our steps, followed the spur we had seen and reached the summit. We had lunch rather late.

Bert got out the map and compass. We had lost a lot of time. Our only way of getting back in time for the train was to take the shorter way down. The way down was steep; the mist persisted making progress very slow.

When we got to the valley floor we met two shepherds who were rounding up sheep. They said they slept in the very small shed we could see; they observed that we were too late for the train, and directed us to their farm some 3 or 4 miles away. We arrived there at about 7pm

Bert told us to wait at the gate while he went to the farm. We were wet, we were cold, we were tired and we were very hungry.

Bert appeared with a very dour farmer. They had a bothy which was kept for stranded walkers. "I don't know what else we can do." We didn't know that he was joking. Our hearts sank.

We were invited into the large living room with a roaring fire and enormous table. We were told the children were in bed. We took off our wet clothing which the farmer's wife took to dry. The table was laid and after many journeys to the kitchen the table was loaded with food.

We all ate heartily, I think there were eight of us. The four youngest slept in the bothy bed – two at the top, two at the bottom, Bert and another lad slept in two large armchairs. The remaining two of us said we would sleep on the hearthrug. The farmer's wife would not hear of it and rolled a feather mattress downstairs. Ray and I had a very comfortable night.

Wherever we went on our summer holidays to Scotland, Bert frequently arranged for us to have a 'Civic reception'. In 1951 we visited Inverness, where we met Provost J.M. Grigor.

Next morning we were awoken about 5.30 by preparations for breakfast. We ate a marvellous cooked meal. On asking what were in debt for their hospitality the farmer told Bert there was no charge and it had been a pleasure to have us. We all subscribed to a collection for the children, collected our warm dry clothes and walked the two miles to Blair Atholl to get the train to Pitlochry.

When we got to Pitlochry and started walking into town, Bert in front half turned to tell us not to look too happy as the main party who had stayed in town would be worried; but Bert tripped and almost fell, which set us off in roars of laughter.

Back at the church hall where we were staying, Ernie, Bert's brother, who had stayed with the rest of the party, said the police had been out all night looking for us. We went to the police station to offer our apologies. There was no telephone at the farm in those days.

On Bert's holidays so many facets of human nature were tested. In addition to Bert's wonderful example, faith and spirituality you never forgot the beauty of the country, the rivers, the lakes, the mountains and all the memories that remain.

RT

Nights with Bert

'A somewhat odd title perhaps for some thoughts on some of my experiences during my teenage years in the company of Bert Bissell,' writes Jeff Harbach who is a long standing and regular supporter of the Vicar Street YMBC.

'An introduction by a lady school teacher to Vicar St. Church lead me to take part in one of the concerts organised by Ernie Bissell around that time. These were hilarious affairs of song, dance and revues, young people of the Christian Endeavour taking part. Held in the old church hall in the late 1930's and early 40's they were some of the high spots of gloomy wartime evenings.

This introduction to Vicar St, of course not only meant the friendship of Ernie but also of Bert who I suppose was the father figure of the two, both so keen to recruit young people to the various activities of the church.

My first-experiences of *'nights with Bert'* were the weekly Monday night, 'Fireside Meetings' In the old vestry at the back of the church, Christian fellowship was enjoyed by a usually full house of teenage lads warmed by a good old-fashioned fire on winter nights.

When the air raids started in earnest 'fire watching' became a must at night for every able-bodied person. I was recruited by Bert to take my turn to look after the church premises.

I have vivid recollections of meeting at night after tea with Bert in the old vestry which was the warmest and most comfortable spot to spend the long night.

On one occasion, I recall an air raid started early and I finished up running to Vicar Street, with the anti-aircraft guns already making a racket on the hill at Oakham nearby.

With a wood fire and blinds carefully drawn we started our nights' vigil. The first few hours would pass by quite quickly. Bert always had books and a fund of excellent tales and experiences. He had the knack of being able to chat on all kinds of subjects, not least of course his mountaineering experiences.

I have only vague recollections of how we snatched a few hours of sleep. I think we had some sort of camp bed, very hard, uncomfortable and cold after about 2am when the fire had died.

Possibly the worst part was getting up, bleary eyed, and going home at dawn for breakfast and then off to school. Fortunately I was never called upon to use the stirrup pump and fire sand buckets.

Holidays with Bert were always eventful. My first experience was a mountain climbing week in the Lake District. Bed invariably meant sleeping on the floor with as much bed clothing as we could struggle with on the train journey. My recollection of that particular first holiday was struggling to get comfortable on the hard floor after a tiring day. For some reason that holiday recalls that when everything was still and quiet in the village, we had a fund of ghost stories recounted by Bert and I think Arthur Roe was often shivering with fright before falling asleep.

The floorboards of the average school or church hall where we were usually billeted seemed about the hardest places on earth. But the influence of Christian comradeship inaugurated by Bert on all these holidays was the most important thing. Looking back I now recognise his extra-ordinary ability to befriend and lead a motley collection of teenagers to bring out the best in each personality.

Bert was of course a leader by example – always out in front on the most tortuous mountain climb, urging on the weakest members.

I recall him on another occasion demonstrating his sporting ability. We had arranged a football match with the local team somewhere in Scotland when our resident goalkeeper Robin Bratt was forced to withdraw at the last minute with an injury. Bert took his place in goal at the ripe old age of forty something. Although we lost something like 5-0 only he prevented a score line of more like 20-0 with a superb exhibition of goal keeping. Needless to say he was nursing a few extra aches and pains next day, no hot baths there to soothe things in those days.

My final memory of a *'night with Bert'* was on the occasion of a long weekend in London. Quite a crowd of us spent the night in the basement of one of Methodism's large city mission halls. We settled down on the floorboard beds, but about half an hour after 'lights out' we were abruptly shaken by a loud crunching noise as the ceiling covering partially disintegrated. Many of our party were covered with debris and dry paint no doubt caused by a combination of body heat and moist air.

Virtual panic in the darkness was avoided as Bert swiftly took command. I can recall his words, 'steady lads, nothing to worry about' as we choked on the plaster and dust. After the initial shock and cleaning up we could all see the funny side.

No one suffered more than a mouthful of dust. I suppose the church custodians were faced with the cost of repairs after our visit but I am sure that Bert used his natural ability to pacify all concerned.

These events now seem distant after the intervening years but for all that, they remain vivid to myself and a memory of a remarkable man with whom I was privileged to have been associated.'

JH

'The Fireside' – the shape of things to come

At one time Methodist Ministers (as well as clergy from all churches) were trained in theology, biblical languages, and church history, but rarely received any training in the pastoral care of people. Arthur Whale, one of those who went into the ministry of the church, reminds us of Bert's tremendous natural ability in this direction in his recollections about earlier days at the Fireside.

'The day that Bert Bissell called at my home when he had heard that I was not attending any church altered the whole course of my life although I was not to realise it until some years later.

It was at the Monday evening meeting of the Fireside in the tiny room known as The Institute the I gave my life to Jesus Christ that marked the beginning of my growth in the Christian faith. It was there that I gave my first Address - it had 32 points! I spent hours of preparation on it, but that is how we were all introduced to public speaking. Many others could give the same testimony.

Bert Bissell was an expert in Pastoral Visitation. I was privileged to accompany on many evenings when he invited me to join him.

He showed me the technique of opening a conversation with people he did not know very well when visiting their home. He would open a conversation, not about Christianity, but by glancing round the room and picking on a photograph, or a cat, or a dog. So, "Is that your brother (or sister, or mother or father)?" Or, "I see you like cats (dogs)". He would chat on about it and make them feel at home with him. None of this, 'Are you saved brother' business.

His approach was gentle and tactful. It was a technique I often used later on when I was in the Ministry - it never failed to work. Another secret about Bert Bissell was his love of hill walking. I shall always be indebted to him for the days out in Wales before the War when I was introduced to the joys of hill walking and later on the holidays in Scotland. When I served as minister in the North some years later my wife and I toured Scotland each holiday for our seven years there. We toured it from north, south, east and west; they were the happiest years of holidays we ever spent. So that is another debt of gratitude I owe to Bert.

There is so much more I could tell. He was a living Saint and, as a Saint should be, utterly sensible. He lived to serve others.'

AW

First impressions

Many people when they first met Bert were struck by characteristics that left an indelible mark.

The man with big boots and a large heart of love for his Master

'A group of us were preparing for an Easter mission, based on a large Church in Leigh-on-Sea. One member of the group suggested that, as part of the preparation, we should take advantage of the visit to Cambridge of a party from Vicar Street, Dudley. Their leader, Bert Bissell, had much to offer on the theme of evangelism. I remember being a bit sceptical - the Lord forgive me - but I turned up at the meeting out of loyalty to a friend. I had heard through Alan Davies of Bert, and was intrigued, in spite of my scepticism.

I remember nothing of the meeting except Bert himself. I was overcome by the phrases he used, his slightly quaint style, his large boots - or so they seemed - his gentle courtesy and his sureness of touch. He was himself, and he knew what he was doing in evangelism. The results of his evangelism are perceptible in the vocations to the ministry of a number of young men. And he referred at crucial moments in his address to 'that Young Man from Galilee', saying the phrase with a quiet passion.'

Revd. Christopher Hughes Smith, a former President of Conference

More big boots - the incessant visitor

Bert was always out and about – visiting people, attending to his work as a Probation Officer, attending events, and taking preaching appointments. It is inevitable that many knew him because of his constant involvement with people at all kinds of level. The following contribution illustrates this. It begins with first impressions and goes on to show some of the ways in which Bert related to all kinds of people.

Kim's parents' house for a considerable time, became a handy hospitality point for entertaining visitors who had travelled to ' The Class' from a distance.

'I grew up across the road from 'Bert Bissell's Church' and must have been about six years old when the fascination began. He'd stand at our porch door, all big boots and fastened up overcoat, ruddy face and effortless twinkle asking: "Is your Dad in?"

This would happen every few weeks, exactly the same pattern: Big Boots at the door, Dad called, Dad and Big Boots had serious pow-wow, Mom called. More talking, occasionally over a cup of tea and a Bourbon in the front room, but usually on the porch step because Big Boots was off to do something else very important.

I'd stand by our black and white silver star-spangled cocktail bar (very posh in the '60s) and watch the ensuing panic as Big Boots left the building.

"But what's he going to think, coming to OUR house?" Mom would say.

"Well Bert wouldn't call if he didn't think we were good enough," Dad would say.

"But will he want a sandwich, or will he only want a piece of cake and a cup of tea?" she'd cry.

"Do both, just in case," Dad said.

A couple of days after this great panic, I'd be in my Sunday best dress, the front room would sparkle and there'd be fresh disinfectant down the toilet, just in case 'the visitor' needed to go. I'd hear the organ playing and go and sit on the front wall, white socks dangling, to see the men coming out of church. Big Boots would be at the gate, shaking everyone's hand as they left. He'd glance up and see me and we'd nod at each other, though he would never wave or gesture in a way that most people would to a child. I thought it very observant of him to realise I didn't particularly like childish behaviour. When most of his 'young men' had departed, he'd gather the 'hangers on' into an orderly group and lead them the few yards to our house like an officer taking his men 'over the top.'

In our front room, the men would talk to Dad, compliment Mom on her sandwiches and do the kid chat thing with me. It was some years before I realised why this seemingly pleasant front room ritual caused my Mom such panic. These men who had laughed and joked their way through Sunday afternoon tea with us were very, very important people indeed, (*politicians, sportsmen, explorers, pilots, international religious leaders, many of whom came via the Missionary Colleges at Selly Oak, Ed.*). It would be impossible to list all the people who visited, but three that come to mind at the moment are Jack Holden, the world champion Cross Country Runner, Duncan Edwards the footballer, and the Rt. Revd. Leonard Wilson, Bishop of Birmingham, formerly Bishop of Singapore. Many of them invariably used our frantically bleached toilet and all because Big Boots said so. But why? What was this power he had to unite people and bring them to Dudley?

By the time I was about eleven, he'd taken to shaking my hand too. I saw this as a great sign of recognition, and almost gave him a hug the first time. But I didn't. Were you allowed to hug Big Boots? He was so different from anyone else I knew that he actually bothered me. He had this warm, radiant glow that drew you in, yet at the same time acted as an impenetrable force field to keep you out.

By now I was attending his church. There were quite a few of us teenagers taking a pew, much to the displeasure of some of the hat-wearing brigade. They seemed to delight in criticising our clothes, our choice of music and our apparent ease at declaring we were at one with the Lord. But Big Boots took it

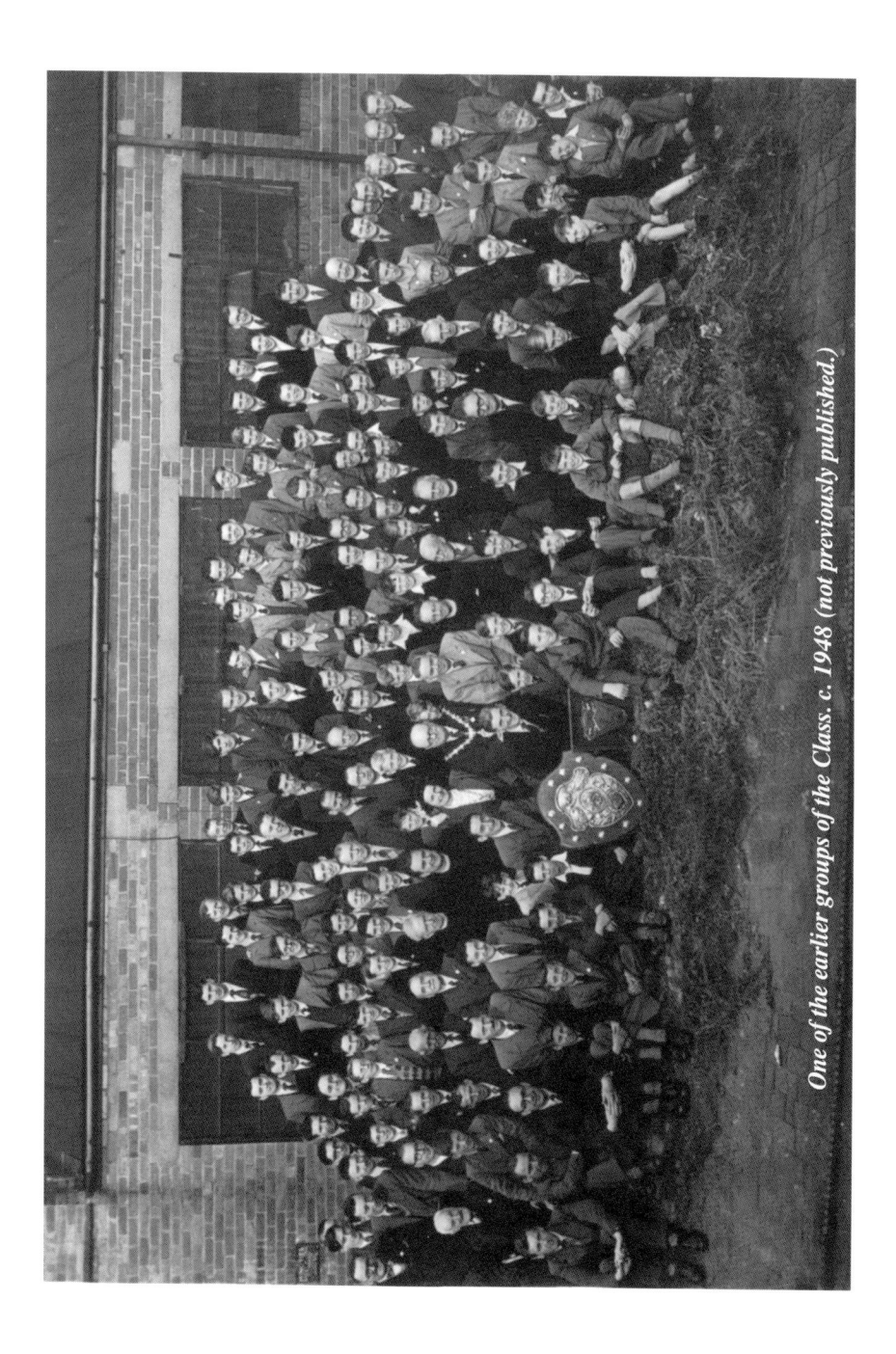

One of the earlier groups of the Class. c. 1948 (not previously published.)

all in his long, purposeful, laid-back stride. He almost seemed to like us. I felt that he was analysing us as much as we were analysing him.

I'd always had a vivid imagination, and this charismatic, enigmatic, yet almost reclusive man made it work overtime. I was very intrigued by his treatment of women. He obviously held them in great esteem as cake-makers and homemakers, and was undoubtedly very respectful towards them. Take my Mom for example: he trusted her to look after all of the Very Important People who addressed the class from year to year. "But does he only trust her as a cake-maker?" I'd ask myself.

This was the age of women's liberation yet he still only took boys on his annual pilgrimage to Ben Nevis. Why was that? Did he think women were inferior and subservient - or was he scared of us? Now there was a new twist!

In my overworked teenage mind I fancied that he was in fact the victim of unrequited love, that he had once encountered a young woman with the same fire in her belly that he had, and she'd chosen God over him. Well, it kept me amused through many a sermon anyway.

Surprisingly enough, we never sat down and had a heart to heart about his views on women, the meaning of life or who it was who'd broken his heart. We got by on handshakes and the odd sideways glance.

It was on the first day of my first real job that I came anywhere close to having an answer. I'd decided that my inquisitive nature should be put to good use and had gained a place as a trainee reporter on the local newspaper. The first day of any job is a nerve-racking experience, but believe me, a newspaper office to an 18 year-old is an awesome place. I didn't even know what to do with a typewriter!

After several attempts at writing a paragraph about a flower show, then watching the news editor turn the air blue, I was feeling that maybe this wasn't the career for me. The 'phone rang, and one of the senior reporters said, "You're wanted in reception. Somebody's got a story for you." I was sure there had been some mistake. "No, he says he only wants to talk to you."

The editor thrust a notebook at me. "You must be OK if you've got stories coming in already," he said. And off I went down the stairs to reception, scared to death in case it was all a big office joke on the new kid.

There he stood, Big Boots and fastened up overcoat, ruddy face and effortless twinkle. "I have a story for you to put in your newspaper," he said.

I didn't get any more than the story - no nudge and wink and "...just thought I'd make you feel good on your first day..." type of remark. He obviously remembered I didn't like childish stuff. He just told me, matter of fact, that I would be his press correspondent from then on, thank you very much, and I would be very good at it. Oh, how I wanted to hug him. The self-esteem he gave me on that day, just by being there, turned it into one from which to rise, not run away.

And let's face it, that was the power he had. The hold he had over people was the ability to make the humble feel important and the important humble. He was an equaliser of men (and women!), regardless of their age, colour or background.

These days I find it very difficult to have faith in religion, but I still believe in God and good, and have a great faith in people. And Big Boots truly was one of God's Good People.

Kim Fuller

Meeting Bert at the Methodist Conference [2]

Revd. Eric Challoner sent us this material from his book and we're very pleased to use it.

'One of the most remarkable men that I ever met came from Dudley, and his name is Bert Bissell. I was a ministerial representative at the Methodist Conference in Sheffield in July 1980.

It was rather a hot afternoon, and I decided to leave the conference hall and go to the refreshment room for a cup of tea. There were not many people in there at the time, but I noticed an old fellow who looked as though he had wandered in from the street hoping to get a cup of tea.

'It so happened' that I decided to go and sit by him and have a chat. Little did I realise just what would be the outcome of that decision.

As I sat down I said, 'Do you mind if I come and sit by you?'

He stretched out his hand and said, 'Please do, my name is Bert and I come from Dudley'.

I replied, 'My name is Eric and I come from Cheadle in Staffordshire'.

Then began a most animated and interesting conversation with Bert doing all the talking.

He told me that his father had been a Methodist minister, and that he had been a Probation officer before his retirement, and that his main interest in life was his Bible Class, in the Vicar Street Methodist Church in Dudley. That does not sound very exciting, but to hear Bert talk about it was. He began the class in 1925, and sixty five years later it was still going strong, and that during this period over twenty members of the class had become ministers. But what was the secret for the success of the class. Without doubt it was Bert himself, and his love for his Bible and his ability to make it alive and relevant for today.

He told me how in one of his studies the subject was mountains, and how they decided that they would have a holiday together climbing the highest mountain in Britain- Ben Nevis. On the top of the mountain they found such a wonderful peace, and at the bottom in the town of Fort William they found a group of Christians with whom they became very friendly, and who like them had climbed Ben Nevis, and found a peace there.'

EC

'He challenged- even in his nineties'
From Karl Khan who is Church Steward at Marlborough Road Methodist Church, St. Albans.

I did not meet Bert Bissell until the summer of 1997, when he was already well advanced in years, aged 93. It was the occasion of David Monkton's formal 'retirement' from his full-time Ministry, at Marlborough Road Church in St Albans, and a celebration of David's 65th birthday. Bert was a special guest and speaker at that 'coming of age' of one of his lads who had made good, as so many of 'his lads' had. I had heard some stories of Bert through David, and had read the book of tributes paid to him by 'his lads' which had been published for his 90th birthday;[3] and so I considered it an honour and a privilege to meet the man at last.

I was greatly impressed, to say the very least, but the lasting impression he made upon me was that - even at that age – he was still challenging and encouraging others.

I had been asked to say a few words at David's farewell gathering, but those few words were sufficient for Bert to say to me on that occasion, "You should be a local Preacher, you know!"

Karl Khan

Dudley's 'First' Probation Officer

Bert was probably more widely known in his middle years as Dudley's first full time Probation officer. There are not many around who worked alongside him at that time. It is easy to forget that Bert had been retired from his probation work for over 30 years when he died.

Ivan Homer sends us a fascinating cutting from the Methodist Recorder in 1989, which recorded that a special ceremony had taken place at the garden shed in Selbourne Road on the occasion of Bert's 87th birthday, but this is no ordinary garden shed It served as the Dudley's probation office for ten years before and during the war.

The shed had been restored by Community Service workers operating under court orders. At this event, the Mayor, Mrs. Celia Hough joined the chief probation officer for the West Midlands, Mr. Eric Morrell to acknowledge the great work Bert had done for the Probation Service. Bert had retired 22 years before!

We have however also received the following items written specifically by people who knew him particularly well in the role of probation officer.

'A personal tribute to a good friend'

'I first met Bert Bissell shortly after 10 a.m. on Monday, 27th November 1961 on my being sworn in to the office of Constable in the former Dudley Borough Police.

I appeared before Dudley Magistrates, and upon leaving the witness box I was met by a man who held out his hand as a gesture of warmth. This person welcomed me to Dudley Police, he said that he felt sure that I had made the right decision in choosing to be a Constable in Dudley and he felt sure that I would do exceptionally well in the Police Force. This man I later discovered was Bert Bissell, the Principal Probation Officer for Dudley.

As the years passed I developed what I can only describe as a special relationship with Bert. Whilst patrolling on the beat he would approach me, ask me how I was doing and other general comments from which a sense of friendship and warmth were to abound.

Bert Bissell was a particular kind of person who found it difficult to find bad in anyone. I recall one particular case before Dudley Quarter Sessions, before the Recorder Gilbert Griffiths, when a local character was appearing before the court for sentence, having been committed by the Magistrates Court. This local character had no fewer than 118 previous convictions and it was clear that the Recorder was at some disadvantage in deciding what to do with him. Bert Bissell was called to the witness box and asked what on earth could

27

be done with this offender. Mr. Bissell told Recorder Griffiths that he honestly felt that if the offender was given one more chance, then he as a Probation Officer might be able to help. Recorder Griffiths queried whether anything could be done with someone who had already had 118 previous chances.

Bert Bissell simply smiled and said *"Sir, please give him one more chance."* This the Recorder did, by placing the offender on a further period of Probation.

In the late 1980's I returned to Dudley having been appointed Superintendent and within 2 or 3 days of my arrival at Dudley I received a visit from Bert Bissell, who promptly welcomed me back to Dudley. This meeting led to my attending a Sunday afternoon Bible Class meeting at Dudley's Vicar Street Methodist Church where I was invited to speak as "Guest Speaker".

My friendship with Bert Bissell was important to me and I had the pleasure of presenting him with a walking stick with a horned handle, which he intended to use on his many walks.

I retired from Dudley Police in 1992 and Bert Bissell, along with so many other good friends, attended Dudley Police Station for my farewell. He was indeed a sincere and most dependable person who's friendship I shall cherish. "They are rich who have true friends"-Fuller.

Roger H Bagley

'Charming, dedicated, fair but firm'

Ernest Edwards, ex law clerk of the Crown Prosecution service first met Bert Bissell in 1966 and remembers him as 'a charming, dedicated Probation Officer,' who impressed him with his fairness when speaking up for his clients to ask the court to place them on probation.

'But he was also unforgiving to those who let him down by breaking their probation, and he seldom asked the Recorder to give them a second chance unless he thought they would deserve it. He was very much respected by everyone involved in the work of the Quarter Sessions, including the office staff, the police, the solicitors and their law clerks.'

EE

'He was my role model'

Leonard W. Lloyd writes

'I write these words as a Retired Probation Officer who knew Bert Bissell for many years.

I am 74 years of age and I first became acquainted with Bert when I was an early teenager, so I knew him for 60 years.

As a youngster I lived on the Watson's Green Estate in Dudley, and to us young lads Bert was a familiar sight when, mounted on an old bicycle, he made his professional 'home visits' around our locality.

Thankfully none of my particular group had ever been in trouble with the Police, but this did not stop Bert taking time out from his busy schedule to dismount from his trusty two-wheeled steed and pleasantly converse about our young lives, current activities etc. Most people got to know and respect Bert Bissell in this way, and the impression he made was lasting.

With the contingencies of the Second World War, and the ups and downs of subsequent resettlement, some years elapsed before I met Bert again, but that next meeting was not accidental. At the time I was in secure but somewhat boring employment, and I had a yen to seek work of a more fulfilling nature.

With this in mind I remember going to have a chat with Bert in his small Probation Office, then situated within Dudley's court buildings, and the fact that he was having a break with a cup of tea and a frugal snack did not reduce the usual warmth of a Bert Bissell welcome. I sought his advice and comment about probation work, something which had been in my mind for some time. Although Bert was quite objective with his comments, and made no attempt to sway me one way or the other, I am sure that it was his personal example of service to others which eventually led me to enter the Probation Service.

In truth it could be said that my early contacts with Bert constituted, in total, a major contributory factor in my choice of career. It would be difficult to find a more committed Christian than was Bert Bissell during his wonderful life and work - he had more faith in his little finger than many professed Christians have in their whole body. I consider it a great privilege to have known him.

I visited Bert in hospital following the unfortunate accident which resulted in that hospitalisation, and from which he never really recovered. I suggested to Bert that he might have felt it ironic that, after over 100 safe ascents of Ben Nevis, that he should have sustained injury on the steps of his own chapel. With a glint in his eye he turned to me and said - " God moves in mysterious ways ". On reflection, I could not have expected any other reply from the incomparable Bert Bissell.'

LWL

As remembered by Ex 'PC 95'

Charlie Davenport recalls an incident in the mid-sixties when he was a police constable 'in what was then Dudley Borough Police. Bert was the borough probation officer. Then the borough was very much smaller with a population of around 66,000.

One day on parade were informed that four properties (shops) had been broken into in the old Hall Street – now Churchill precinct, and Birdcage Walk, including Crannige and Dentith's shop which at that time also carried a considerable stock of toys as well as picture frames.

Later on in the afternoon I caught two young boys letting off fireworks on waste ground in Kates Hill, who had a stock of toys and fireworks and other property from the shops that had been broken into.

Bert became involved, and later when obtaining a statement from the owner of Crannidge and Dentith, I mentioned that the one boy and his younger brother and sister were very deprived, with terrible home circumstances, even though they really loved their mother. They would probably get nothing for the fast approaching Christmas.

I was asked if there many such children. "Oh, yes!" I replied.

I was then taken to an upstairs room where there were many unsaleable toys - broken, damaged, shop-soiled etc.

The owner said, "If you want them, they are yours for the poor kids!"

I spoke to Bert, who was very pleased but said "I'm not very good at repairing things."

"No problem, I'll show you," I said.

I had an old Morris Minor van then – probably the first one they ever made – and we filled it twice.

Bert and I and others spent many hours sorting out these toys. A lot of children had presents that year they would never have had.

The two boys went to court and were punished. No cautions in those days!

After that Bert started to bring two, three or four needy kids to the Police Christmas Children's Party. This went on for many years.

I was at that time part of the 'Police Singing Quartet'. We used to perform at various functions in the Police Club. Bert heard us, and we were invited to sing at 'Vicar Street,' Bert's domain. When we had done our bit with numerous renditions, I was amazed to see a man who I had locked up for burglary some time before, and who had been 'out' for two weeks taking round 'the plate' – such was Bert's trust in his fellow men whether good or bad.'

CD

Cameos

It seems appropriate at this point to include facets of Bert's life as they appeared to other people on a whole variety of different subjects.
The first piece has travelled quite a distance!

The 'Fine' fellow

'I was a bit young to know much about Bert Bissell really. My big brother David was the one who mainly talked about Bert; he even cycled all the way to Inverness once in the 1950's to join the group who climbed Ben Nevis.

Often when I use the term 'I'm fine', it takes me back to meeting Bert, usually somewhere in New Road, Dudley. This imposing figure of a man would come striding down the pavement wearing a dark overcoat, trilby sort of hat and swinging a walking stick. I never did now whether he really needed the walking stick, or was it a theatrical prop?

"Hallo, my fine young fellow" he would say to me. "And how is Dayvid?"(It always sounded somewhat nasal the way he said it).

The first climb up Ben Nevis in 1936. Sidney Dando (left) Bert (right)

"He's fine" – I would say.
"And your father? What a great fellow he is"
"He's fine as well"
"Now you make sure that you remember me to them both."

The on his way he would go, leaving me to think what does he mean by 'fine'? This kind of exchange happened several times until I was old enough to ride by cycle on the road, then the greeting turned to a cheery wave – we didn't need to use words.

So now when someone asks me how I am, I tell them, "I'm fine."
So you see there is a little bit of BB around in New Zealand too!

Bruce Monkton, Auckland New Zealand.

'Visiting Schools'

Bert had a very wide network of contacts with young people. Many of us came to meet him first of all through his contacts with local schools. Later in his life he was a very popular speaker in schools and colleges, not only about his work for peace, but because of his age and ability as a captivating speaker – even to within eighteen months of his death – he was in demand as a speaker to children on a whole range of subjects relating to life. It was very appropriate that a children's choir, from Milking Bank Primary School - one of the schools he regularly visited - should sing at his thanksgiving memorial service at the town hall.

Tony Willis, Deputy Headteacher of Castle High School St. James's Road Dudley touches on many aspects of his earlier contacts with schools.

'I first came into contact with Bert as a schoolboy playing soccer for the first XI at Dudley Grammar School - this figure would loom out of the mists of the far side of the playing field, and, in what seemed only a few gigantic strides, he would be on the touchline adding encouragement for the team. He was a regular visitor for the games and would even come on the coach to away games.

When I first married I lived near to Bert and would meet him regularly and talk for long periods - he showed interest in my career and that of my wife (there were many 'requests' to Jan in the coming years to bring her school choirs to Vicar Street!)

After teaching in a couple of local authorities I was appointed to a job within Dudley and Bert became involved with the school - attending plays, speech days, presentation mornings and dance festivals (on one occasion he attended the morning dance display, left and walked to Lower Gornal for an appointment and walked back to school in time for the afternoon display!)

I thought that it would be a good idea to try to let some pupils take part in a 'climb' up Ben Nevis with Bert, this turned out to be the last year that Bert successfully climbed the Ben. We travelled up to Fort William by minibus (my wife and 2 sons and 9 pupils); we had to be in Fort William by 5pm as Bert had arranged tea with civic dignitaries to thank us for taking part in the walk! We slept on the floors of a church hall and a scout hut and then met the next morning with a large group of other walkers to climb Bert's beloved Ben Nevis.

The weather was superb and Bert talked to the whole group before starting the climb. On the way up Bert had to take regular rests and received treatment for many bouts of cramp - his progress was also hindered by requests from other people on the Ben for photographs to be taken with him, everyone recognised him.

At the top of the Ben it was still covered by 4 metres of snow - the peace cairn could not be seen - neither could Bert, as he had still not arrived at the summit even after a couple of hours after the rest of us.

It was arranged that a service would be held and people were beginning to think that Bert would not make it, when something magical happened. Over the brow of the mountain, set against a brilliant blue sky and shining white snow came this stooped figure flanked by two mountain rescue men, Bert walking with the aid of a walking staff appeared to come right out the pages of a picture of biblical times.

With the arrival of Bert everything suddenly started to happen - he pointed out exactly where the peace cairn was buried by snow and the service was held directly above it.

The return down the mountain was a pleasant journey and a tired, but very happy group returned to their floors in the 2 halls to collapse! Bert took until 1030 p.m. to return to Fort William!

The following morning at about 7.45, the door to the scout hut was rapped and I slowly moved to open it - slowly because I was aching so much from the exertions of the day before. Greeting me was a tanned gentleman looking very spry - Bert- he just wanted to know if I would take a case back to Dudley for him as he was going on to another visit before returning home. After handing the case to me he turned and walked quickly away without any sign of aching!

Bert Bissell was a very unique person, he had the ability to make every individual feel important and very special and he had an aura about him that made him stand out in any gathering. It was a great privilege to know Bert Bissell and a great experience to have shared time with him and to see his magical effect on people of all ages. He will be long remembered - the school will be taking a group of pupils to Fort William to climb the Ben every Whitsun from 1999 to help maintain the traditions and beliefs that were so dear to Bert.'

Many think of Bert as relating to men only. When the need arose however, he was able to show adeptness and 'versatility.'

TW

One person cannot change the world, but...

In January 1975 our daughter was hit by a car on her way to school. 'Mr. Bissell' visited the hospital within hours. Bearing in mind that Bert worked and lived in an almost exclusively male world, it was not easy undertaking to sit by the bedside of a 12-year old girl who had just been flung through the windscreen of a car, Bert was not one to shirk any task. He did not need modern day parenting skills or trauma counselling to show compassion.

If a job description for being a Christian was required I would think that total loyalty, the duty of care, and complete commitment would be necessary qualifications. Bert was in possession of all these.

I very rarely go to Church, but although he did not always remember my name, Bert always knew when I attended one of his Bible Class 'specials.' Much more importantly, he always knew when I wasn't there - it was a comforting feeling to realise you had been missed!

One person cannot change the world, but the world for one person can be changed, and I think Bert Bissell did this on many occasions.

Doreen Wedge

(Many people's ears must have burned over the years with the words, 'We missed you on Sunday.' Ed.)

A Baptists view

Mr. J. Brooks recalls. 'I have known our brother and friend, Bert Bissell since the early thirties, when he canvassed Netherton, the area where I lived, for young men to join the vicar Street Bible Class. Although I'm a Baptist by reason of my upbringing, I recall many times visiting Vicar Street for the Lantern Slides in my younger days.

Bert to me is like the apostle Paul, who was all things to all men that he might win some for Christ… A truly amazing man who gave God all the glory. Our prayers should be that God would send labourers into his vineyard of the same calibre as Bert Bissell.'

JB

From a Temperance Society worker

'I have a happy memory of Bert Bissell. In 1934 my friend and I joined the Temperance Society. It was a children's club which was held in a room over a milliners shop in the upper High Street in Dudley. We went to camp at Asley Burf for a week's holiday. The week before Mr. Bissell brought his magic lantern to show slides of the camp. He then spent time with us at the camp. It's a week we never forgot.'

Freda Parkes

'Fireside Instruction'

'On Monday evenings' writes Alan, 'we would meet for our Fireside Class. It was in this meeting that the young teenagers met and were given their first introduction to speaking and preaching.

One night, we asked Bert why as a probation officer he could possibly defend someone he knew to be guilty. His reply was to remain with me and act as a guide to me in later years in all my dealings with other people.

Bert said, "We are bound to judge acts. Stealing is wrong. We are bound to judge attitudes. Envy is wrong, hate is wrong. But only God can judge people, because only he can know all the facts about them – their pain, their childhood weaknesses and temperament – all the things that have gone towards making them what they are."

This is why Bert looked for the good in everyone.'

Alan Wedge – Group Class Leader.

A 'One World' person

Bert Bissell was truly a One World person because of his church and community work and his witness for world peace. In the early days of Dudley One World he brought some friends from Hiroshima and the Lochaber Pipe band to take part in an Open Day and parade in Dudley town centre. He attended many of our events until shortly before he died and we are proud to have been associated with him.

George Cloke –Dudley's One World Week Organiser.

'He lived just round the corner'

'I lived just round the corner from Mr. Bissell for thirty four years,' writes Mrs. Townsend. 'He came to our house the very first week we moved in. My family of boys wasn't very old so they sort of grew up with him. My youngest son went up Ben Nevis and one year Mr. Bissell gave him the honour of laying the wreath on the summit for him.

To me, he wasn't just and neighbour and friend, he was a father figure always being there when I needed him. Fourteen years ago I lost my husband, he had been ill with cancer for twelve months. Mr. Bissell never missed a day from coming to see him, always bringing a bit of fruit, chocolate or even a bunch of flowers trying his hardest to cheer my husband. When he eventually passed away he was the truest friend I could have had; he practically arranged almost everything.

My lads all played football and every Saturday afternoon Mr. Bissell and myself were always there to watch them, someone always took us in their car even when they were playing away. One Saturday afternoon they were playing the Cup round at Wordsley Park. We were thrilled to bits when they won it. He was like a young lad going round to each of the lads congratulating them – smiles all over his face.

This Christmas is going to be very hard for us, because in all the thirty four years we were all old pals, this will be the very first time he is not here with us to exchange Christmas cards and presents.

For weeks before Christmas I would study a poem to write in his card because loved poetry. As a matter of fact each time he went to Scotland, I would write him one to put through his door, a little bit of a welcome home for him if you like to call it that. I visited him one day when he had been poorly and he got them all out of the cupboard, he had kept them all.

The last time I saw him was when they took him to hospital. I wrote to the Queen to ask if should would send him a get-well message. I got that message from her. I know how much he admired Her Majesty. When I gave him the letter his face shone, but I am afraid he was nearer to God than I thought, he died a few days later. I went to Vicar Street Church the afternoon of his funeral with tears in my eyes, but in my heart, I felt if anyone was up there with his maker it would be him, and I shall always carry in my memory, a man I was very proud to have known.'

Mrs Townsend

'The telling Sixpence!'

Mrs. Margaret Davies, a retired Community Nursing Sister relates to us an incident told to her by her late husband who in his youth was a member of the Bible Class. Bert used to call regularly at her husband's home regularly on a Friday teatime. 'On one occasion he asked her late husband if he knew who had broken a window nearby. John owned up straight away, and to his surprise Mr. Bissell gave him 6p "for telling the truth."

In later years I myself knew Mr. Bissell in my capacity as a Community Nursing Sister based at Cross Street Clinic, he was my patient on at least two occasions. He was always a perfect gentleman, he walked everywhere, and when he needed treatment at the clinic he always raised his hat to the ladies he met: a trait that is sadly lacking these days. May God Bless one of Dudley's most generous and kindly treasures.'

MD

'Tend to the widow and the fatherless' (James 1 vs 37)

In the month of May 1961, a dear gentleman knocked on my door one Monday evening on behalf of Vicar Street church. He had heard my husband had passed away suddenly. He was most kind and helpful in many ways.

When the football season started, he took my son Paul to Coventry City many times. I often felt that by taking Paul under his wing Bert helped him to come to terms with the loss of his father.

Bert arranged for us, as a family – Julie, Paul and I - to have a wonderful holiday in Scotland, to climb The Ben.

Over the years I always felt that Bert treated everyone as if they were very special, from the schoolboy who had a hole in his shoe, to the man in the posh car.

Whenever we had anything special at church – 'tea parties' we called them, Bert always went back home with a big bag of cakes to last him for a few days. He certainly had a 'sweet tooth!'

Being President of the Ladies class for many years I heard him many times when he came along to our class with such wonderful stories that remained with you for a long time… he always appreciated everything the ladies did for Vicar Street.'

Dorothy Morgan. Dorothy and Sam, her husband, are joint Senior Church Stewards at Vicar Street Church..

Sidney Poitier Y.M.B.C!

Bert often used to advise us to share our faith with others 'through ever increasing circles of friendship.' The thing was that we didn't always realise how wide his own 'circles of friendship' had grown.

Sitting, looking at the collection of photographs that Bert had on display in his front room, I was surprised to see one that looked like Sidney Poitier. Looking more closely I read the inscription 'To Bert, Very Best Wishes, Sidney Poitier.'

How did Bert come to have an autographed photo of a film star? When he came back into the room I asked him.

He told us that he had read a very interesting article that Sidney Poitier had written about racism and because he was very impressed with it, he had written to the actor to congratulate and encourage him.

Bert added. "I also made him an honorary member of 'The Class'."

Sidney Poitier had included the photograph when he had replied to Bert's letter.

Pauline Monkton

The new Class badges

Periodically a new Class badge would be produced, to mark some special anniversary of the Vicar Street Young Men's Bible Class. The design was always the same except that the basic background was enamelled in a different colour.

Our story begins during early June 1994, when, I was taking Bert back home following his visit to the Gentlemen Songsters Monday evening rehearsal. We were just passing the Netherton reservoir, when Bert said, "Harold I have a problem, I am trying to obtain a new set of badges for the class ready for the 70th anniversary celebration". He went on to say " I have tried to locate the whereabouts of the original supplier, but have so far been unsuccessful". As I have a contact in the Birmingham jewellery quarter, I told Bert that I would try to help.

My contact in the jewellery quarter was able to tell me that the company who Bert had been trying to find had gone out of business some time ago, however, he gave me a further contact who had taken their business over. That firm had also ceased to trade and that the business had been taken over by a company in Hereford. I wrote to Bert and passed on this information, suggesting that he send one of the original badges to them to help them to locate the die from which they had been produced (that is if it still existed).

Shortly after this I received a 'phone call from Bert, to thank me in his usual way for what I had done; however the company at Hereford were unable to locate the die. I asked him to give me further time in which I could hopefully locate an alternative source of supply.

Eventually I contacted R.E.V. Gomm's in Frederick Street Birmingham. I 'phoned this company and explained that I was contacting them on behalf of Mr Bert Bissell - they instantly recognised Bert by name and had seen him on the television programme of his journey to Fort William. Messrs Gomm stated

Vicar Street Young Men's Bible Class Mission Band in 1950 (under Bert's leadership). Left to right - front: Alan Wedge, Bill Parkes, Tony Wesson, John Nott; back: Bill Detheridge, David Monkton.

that they would be very pleased to meet Bert and discuss the making of a new die, plus supply of badges from the die.

Again, Bert was full of his usual praise for my efforts, which I considered to far outweigh what I had actually done. It really had been a privilege to assist Bert in just a very small way as this, especially when one compares that to the immense number of good things which Bert did for others throughout his life.

However, a few weeks later I received a 'phone call from Bert,

"What are you doing on Sunday afternoon Harold?"

"Nothing in particular," I replied.

"Good, because I want you to present the new class badges."

Harold R. Eades ('Gentleman Songsters' Male Voice Choir)

Chickens!

Bert had his own sense of humour which wasn't always as clear in its meaning to other people as it might have been!

'It used to be the custom each year after the anniversary meeting of the Vicar Street Bible Class that the ladies would put on a splendid tea in the meeting hall behind the Church. Towards the end of the tea, Bert would get up to propose a vote of thanks to the ladies and then launch into one of his 'humorous stories.' I remember that one of these involved the chickens which his mother had kept in the back garden to provide eggs for the table.

Time came when the hens went off laying and the yield of eggs virtually dried up. Advice was sought from various friends but none was able to put a finger on the cause of the trouble. Things were getting desperate when the name of a professional expert was suggested, one with a high reputation in these matters. In due course the man was contacted and a day fixed for him to pay a visit and examine the birds. It was confidently predicted that he would quickly be able to spot the cause of the problem.

At last the great day came for the visit and all was prepared. The expert arrived and undertook an examination of every aspect of the birds and their circumstances after which the family assembled to hear the pronouncement of his findings.

However the speech was unexpectedly brief and disappointingly unhelpful. He merely announced "There's summat up or summat"

History does not record what happened after that dismissive comment! Doubtless the humour of the situation was less evident to the family at the time than it was to Bert when he recounted it many years later. *Somewhere along the line the connection between the story and punch line had got lost!'*

Derek Vonberg.

The Revd Stuart G. Radford, from Darley Dale, Matlock, illustrates another kind of Bert humour.

The Safe Five pounds!

In 1989 Bert challenged the Wolverhampton and Shrewsbury District to join him on his 101st climb of Ben Nevis. I was then District Local Preachers secretary and responded to his challenge, as did quite a few others including the Chairman, John Sampson, plus wife and dog.

Bert offered £5 to anyone who found his hat on the mountain. Apparently when the BBC filmed his 100th climb, the BBC helicopter had blown his hat off. Needless to say, no-one found the hat. His £5 was safe.'

Stuart also reminds us of *'How unstoppable he was!*

'In 1993, I was a student at Queens College in Birmingham. I invited Bert to come and talk to the students. I was supposed to interview him. That was a joke. I spoke just one sentence and off he went talking at length about his exploits. The only way of stopping him was to say that it was time for college lunch.

In the afternoon I took him down to Blue Coat School. The headteacher there used to be my RE teacher years before and his name was Brian Bissell. I had learned that they were distant relations who had never met. So that afternoon they did, and the boys at the school were also regaled with his stories.'

SGR

And finally in this chapter 'a few words' from Jim Brookes who must be the longest serving member of the Class and for a very long time one of Bert's most loyal helpers and supporters.

Christian Fellowship at its best

'I met Bert at the Class at the age of fourteen. I'm now 86.

I was supposed to be a Christian – C. of E, but when I started work at 14, I could please myself. My friend asked me to go to Bert's Class at Vicar Street Methodist Church, the 'Young Men's Bible Class' two miles walk away from where I lived. I reluctantly accepted the invitation. It was the best move of my life. I converted to Christianity through the influence of Bert.

Bert's Class (then) had a membership of 400 men. Chiefly through Bert, 18 went into the ministry and are working for the Lord several of them are now serving as supernumeraries. I myself was Secretary of the church for 42 years. The quantity of service given to God's work through Bert's influence is immeasurable....

He climbed Ben Nevis 105 times, I'm afraid I only climbed 6 times, but I do know what it's like. To Bert, this was Christian Fellowship at its best... (it's been) Great Christian Fellowship'.

Jim

Ben Nevis, and the Cause of Peace

Bert always felt a sense of guidance in many of the things that he was involved in. This was certainly true of events that came as an outcome of the climbing of Ben Nevis on VJ Day. The following items touch on incidents shared by some of those who shared many stages of this experience with him.

Events leading up to VJ Day

Bob Crew writes:

'It was late July 1945, and I was looking forward to my visit with Bert Bissell to Scotland. I was eighteen and a half at the time, expecting my call up papers for my entry into the Army and horror of horrors they arrived instructing me to enlist the same week as my departure for Scotland.

I sought Bert in his Probation office and explained the situation. He listened attentively and told me to call back in a couple of hours. On my return he explained that he had telephoned someone in the War Office and I had been granted a deferment, and I was given a new date to report for duties after my return from Scotland.

On the journey to Fort William, we were late arriving in the small station of Crianlarich and had missed our connection. We were tired and somewhat disappointed at this unexpected turn of events, but suddenly Bert disappeared taking great strides down the rail track towards the signal box. He returned a few minutes later informing us that, yes; our connection to Fort William had gone. This was the last passenger train of the day, but there was a goods train due in a few minutes and the Signalman had agreed to stop it and we could travel in the guard's van. All worked as planned and we completed our journey at the rear of the goods train – through the winding track and a thunderstorm that was now raging furiously.

It was I think, August the 15th and I, like my colleagues had spent rather an uncomfortable night on the floor of the Church Hall.

We were slowly awakening and still bleary eyed when a loud voice said. "Lads, peace has been declared in Japan, and we shall climb The Ben this morning." Little did I realise that he meant *'now.'*

Mist persisted most of the day, and none of us was very enthusiastic climbing in this weather, but with much encouragement from our leader that, 'we were nearly there' or it was 'just over the top' or 'just round the corner', we finally reached the summit.

The first inscribed stone in the Cairn installed on the fourth anniversary in 1949.'

Bert suggested we build a peace Cairn in memory of VJ Day 1945. We each placed our lump of rock until the small mound was complete, and never shall I forget the eerie silence as he led us in prayer and we stood with heads bowed.

As we descended the mountain, the mists cleared and the sun shone, little did I realise then that my small contribution placed on that peak would be a symbol of peace, spoken of in many parts of the world in years to come.'

BC

The 'whistle stop' tour

Derek Siviter writes.

'I was one of the part Gentlemen Songsters who climbed with Bert and sang on the top of Ben Nevis in July 1978. There were 58 climbers on that day, the youngest, a child of 11 years and the oldest (apart from Bert ed.!) a chorister aged 74, and so it was inevitable that the group should get strung out as the climb wore on.

One of my lasting memories of Bert on that climb was his use of a whistle.

Before we began to climb, Bert explained to us that we would climb so far at a time, then take a rest and on a blast from his whistle start to climb again. So you can imagine what happened!

Bert led the way with his long rangy stride and would bring the leading climbers to a halt when he judged the time right. Just when the last of the puffing perspiring stragglers reached the seated party, Bert would blow his whistle and off we set once more. I firmly believe that there were quite a few climbers who never had a rest in 4,000 feet on that day.'

DS

The Vonberg families' first meeting with Bert

Derek and Barbara Vonberg have been loyal supporters of the class ever since they first met Bert in Fort William many years ago. Their son, the Revd. David H. Vonberg is the Superintendent Minister of the Stockton on Tees Circuit.

'The year was 1967. In August the Vonberg family decided to take the children for a holiday in Scotland to a farm near Fort William. 'On the Sunday morning after arrival we went into the town in search of a church. The first we came to was called Duncansburgh and in we went.

At the end of the Service as the congregation left, we noticed that a group of young people had gathered round the organ and were singing hymns. Thinking that they were some local lads we went up to join in, little knowing what wide ranging experiences would stem from that simple step.

We were instantly welcomed in most encouraging terms by a tall gentleman, evidently their leader. Strangely the voice was West Midland, certainly not Scottish, and the group turned out to be Methodists like ourselves. Thus we were introduced to Bert and members of Vicar Street Bible Class in Dudley.

From then on we were invited to participate in various activities of the Class including walks by Loch Ness, visiting Lord Lochiel, evidently a personal friend of Bert's and of course, climbing the Ben. It was all most exciting for our children aged 18, 15 and 12 and they asked for a repeat performance next year!

I recall one little episode typical of Bert, during a walk on the banks of Loch Ness. Bert as usual was leading the party when another walker approached us from the opposite direction and stopped to speak to Bert. They at once became engaged in deep conversation and I assumed that it was a friend of Bert's from previous visit to the area. When afterwards I asked Bert about the man, the answer was "never seen him before in my life!"

This little incident, I learnt, was typical of Bert who, like John Wesley, would welcome serious conversation with, virtually anyone he met.'

Derek Vonberg

'A masochist or a Methodist?'

Pat Jones tells us

'It was in 1991 when I suddenly had the idea that I would like to go on holiday to Scotland and climb Ben Nevis. My husband Bill, was very surprised, but readily agreed to my suggestion. While we were waiting for the accommodation brochure to arrive Bill, suggested that we make it a sponsored climb to raise funds for the school of a handicapped little boy that we had started taking out each week to give his parents a rest.

We also thought that it would be nice if we could go during the time that

Bert was there with his party of lads. Bill rang Bert to find out when he was going and told him of our plans - Bert was delighted.

About two weeks before we were due to go, Bert telephoned to say he had heard the Queen was visiting Fort William on the Monday following our arrival. His party had been allocated a position on the green outside Duncansburgh Church, and he would be delighted if we would like to join his party for this visit. I was absolutely thrilled as I have always been a fan of the Royal Family and I couldn't wait to get to Fort William.

The great day arrived and although it was raining we were up early. The guesthouse we were staying at overlooked Loch Linnhe and as we went into the dining room for breakfast I was thrilled to see the Royal Yacht *Britannia* already moored in the loch.

Despite the rain we set off after breakfast in high spirits to join Bert in Duncansburgh Church Hall to wait for our instructions. I could not believe it was actually happening. Eventually Bert called us together to go out onto the green, to the place reserved for us. Just before the Queen arrived at the green the rain stopped, as if there had been a signal. Suddenly there was a buzz of excitement and there she was stepping out of her car. She was being escorted round the green when the person escorting her stopped pointed Bert out to her and bought her over to speak to him. I could hardly contain my excitement, because there she was standing talking to Bert, just two feet away from where Bill and I were standing - I had never been so close to Royalty before.

Bert was proudly wearing his medals (his MBE, his Methodist World Peace Medal and his International Rotary Club Medal) and looking just as he always was, quite calm and dignified. I remember Bert telling Her Majesty that he still remembered the occasion when she presented him with his MBE in 1959 and that he had climbed the Ben over 100 times, to which the Queen replied that he must be a masochist, but Bert must have misheard what she said, because when he was relating the conversation later he said that she had said he must be a Methodist!' *(The story goes that Bert, on that occasion, said to the Queen, 'You're doing a wonderful work your majesty.')*

Pat & Bill Jones

The Challenge to Climb the Ben

As the incoming President of Methodist Conference The Revd Christopher Hughes Smith was invited to speak at the Diamond Jubilee Rally in Dudley Town Hall in September 1985. He writes:

'I gave my address, and at some point in the proceedings, Bert issued his challenge. He challenged me as President of the Methodist Conference to climb Ben Nevis with his party on the Wednesday of the following Spring Bank holiday. I smiled and thought that I was safe: the diary for the year was made and additions were almost impossible! The meeting came to a close, and that was that, I thought!

I could not escape however the thought of Bert Bissell's life's mission, I listened to the story of the origin of the climbing The Ben on VE day, as some one said, to keep the members of the Bible Class out of reach of alcoholic ways of celebrating. The building of the Peace Cairn on the summit began. I learned of the letters sent all over the world to climbers of the world's highest mountains to invite them to add a peace message to the things that marked their successful climbs. I realised that the idea was to link the determination, effort and perseverance of climbing a high mountain with the effort necessary for the making of global peace, and that a generation of climbers might begin to see the point. I further saw the possibility that Bert might be inviting the President of the Conference to make the climb so that a new generation of young people might join the struggle for World Peace, seen as a summit for the whole human race.

After a day's rest, we went to the eve of climb preparation meeting at Duncansburgh Church and those assembled began to become a party with a purpose, and to enter into the myth of adventure. We re- assembled, after a very good breakfast, at 9 a.m. on Wednesday morning. Bert was in the lead, and refused to be overtaken. The walk was a long slog at Bert's steady experienced pace. The last two hours of zigzagging up the side of the Ben made the most demands, and unfortunately visibility was very disappointing. However, on the summit, though the cairn was covered with snow, and it was misty, we made a circle and read scripture, offered prayer and sang a hymn. Bert made sure that there was a photograph of the occasion. During the whole of the climb, we felt perfectly safe because of the presence members of the Lochaber Mountain Rescue team, lovely people of huge experience who themselves showed great respect for Bert.'

CHS

'Passport to participation'

Peter Boxley first met 'Mr. Bissell' in 1959 when 'I was a young man of 22 years. I had recently competed in the Ben Nevis mountain race as a member of Tipton Harriers. It was an unusual event for the club to enter and had aroused a lot of interest in the local press.

Mr. Bissell arrived at the Harriers clubhouse with a few colleagues and was very interested in the race and our visit to Fort William. I particularly remember their faces when they saw our 'times'. We all finished in about two and a quarter hours. They told us they spent most of the day up there doing it.

I was invited to Vicar Street to read a passage from the Bible the following week – I think it was the anniversary. I was very nervous about doing this but to this day I'm still proud to say that I did go and I did it.

I, like everyone else I know who had ever met Mr. Bissell, was in his army of admirers.'

PB

The Hiroshima Stone

'Another year we found ourselves once again taking our holidays in Scotland to coincide with the visit of the Class to Fort William. The big event on this occasion was the arrival from Japan via Dudley of the magnificent Hiroshima Stone Tablet. It was to be added to the famous Peace Cairn which Bert had initiated on the summit of the Ben in 1945 to mark the end of the war.

The Stone was of considerable weight and Bert had arranged with the Mountain rescue team for them to take the massive stone to the top for incorporation into the cairn. Bert had organised a special Service on summit of the Ben the next day to mark the occasion. A number of important people had been invited to join a climb and participate in the Service.

Unfortunately, on the morning of the Sunday when the stone was to be taken up, news came through that the Mountain Rescue Team had been out on a rescue during the night and were in no state to carry up the stone!

I have never seen Bert so much put out, and I can remember the look on his face as he came back down the aisle, having just received the news. He looked grim but determined.

His solution was to seek help from students of Nottingham and Sheffield Universities, who were camping near to the Ben. They readily responded to Bert's persuasive approach, formed a team, up went 'the stone' and the visitors' climbed and the Special Service took place as planned.

The spin off was the beginning of a lasting association between Vicar Street Bible Class and students of the two Universities which continued for many years. It is an example typical of the way in which Bert turned a problem into a means of grace and the positive spread of Christian influence'.

Reminiscence by Derek Vonberg

The Hiroshima Cross

But of course, the story of the Hiroshima stone didn't end there as Eric Challoner reminds us from the conversations had taken place between himself and Bert.

He tells us how Bert had related to him that the cairn on Ben Nevis, 'was certainly inspired, for it has now become an International 'War Memorial' and we have built into it a stone from Everest sent by Sir Roger Hunt, a tablet from the Scouts of America, another representing the Youth of the United Nations.'

The one that Bert was most proud of was the Hiroshima Tablet sent by the Junior Chamber of Commerce at the request of the mayor of Hiroshima, Mr. Setsua Yamada, 'a wonderful ambassador of peace' said Bert enthusiastically.

The mayor sent it carefully packed in a wooden crate, and he arranged for the Japanese embassy in London to deliver it to Dudley, where it was consecrated in the Vicar Street Methodist church, and from there transported to Fort William, and with the help of the whole group, taken to the top, and built into the Cairn.

'It so happened' that when they collected the tablet from the church in Dudley, two pieces of the wooden crate were accidentally left behind.

The Vicar Street Prayer group looked at these two pieces of wood from Hiroshima and decided to have them made into a cross and to call it *The Hiroshima Cross*.

The head of the woodwork class of the local school undertook to be responsible for this. Then Bert took it to Coventry Cathedral, where it was consecrated, and placed in their Chapel of Unity, with the understanding that it could be used in different places where peace was the theme.

I was thrilled just to listen to Bert, and in a very short time felt that I had known him all my life. It was time to get back into the Conference hall, and as I left him he said 'Brother Eric, if you would ever like to use this cross at any time let me know.' It so happened that I had been booked to speak at an Ecumenical service in the parish church at Cheadle on Armistice Sunday that year, and would be glad to take the cross. Bert readily agreed, and so in November of that year, he together with his precious cross arrived at Crewe Station, and came to our Manse with it. What a delightful guest he was.'

EC

'He got to the top'

Ron Marriott recalls the impressive way Bert spoke to young people in Wolverhampton about his visit to the Holy Land in 1975: how he had been in the 'Shepherds Fields' in Palestine, and how everyone felt they had been there with him. His style of speaking in itself left an indelible mark in people's minds.

He also remembers one of Bert's last journeys up 'the Ben' in May 1992 when there was two or three feet of snow around the cairn. 'This was the day,' he records, 'when Bert made it to the top with help of guides and I understand it took him around 13 hours, but he was determined not to give up. He seemed as fresh as ever the next morning. This was the only occasion when the owner of the top half of the Ben climbed to the top.'

RM

The President of what?

The Revd Nigel Gilson, President of the Methodist Conference 1986-87, writes:

'I enjoyed being Bert Bissell's Chairman in the Wolverhampton & Shrewsbury District from 1975 to 1988. He was always most courteous and gracious to all his colleagues in the Church, and that was true of his attitude to everyone. He won great respect for his work in the Probation Service, in Racial Equality activities and in the community generally. His outstanding service of the Vicar Street Bible Class was specially marked by his pastoral care for all its members.

One of my very special joys was to share the climb of Ben Nevis in 1987. If

I had had any reservations about going, his enthusiasm and personal example, at well beyond my age, would have dispelled them.

In the event I would not have missed it.

I still chuckle as I recall his special concern for me as 'President of Conference,' With his usual care he shepherded us all up the mountain, urging all the walkers, Methodist and others, "Keep behind the President. Don't go ahead of the President. The President must be in front" with an almost embarrassing deference!

When we paused for coffee I found myself sitting beside one of the boys from the local school, who were with him as usual. As we chatted, he asked me in his delightful Scots accent, with a mixture of politeness and curiosity,

"Pardon me, Sir, but what are you President **of**?"

That has remained an amusing memory of the special occasion, still recorded in a large photograph of us at the Ben, generously given me by Bert, a precious souvenir, which hangs prominently above our stairway. It was a highlight of an exciting year.

THANK YOU, BERT.

Nigel L Gilson

'Climbing another mountain'

We do not have report about all the mountains that Bert climbed, or the consequences of these climbs in terms of relationships that he made over the years but Derek Bissell, one of Bert's nephews tells of Bert's visit at the age of 80 to Australia after 'having an open invitation from us for years.'

'The highlight of the trip was to climb Mt. Kosciusko in the Snowy Mountains about 250 miles south-west of Sydney. A peace message was to be placed on the summit. This is Australia's highest peak and stands at 7,346 feet. We planned to spend a week in the area and were based in Cooma, a town about 60 miles from the mountain. Initially Bert with his natural flair for the big occasion wanted me to organise a march up to the summit with a band etc., but I was able to dissuade him from this stressing the necessity for a low-key approach.

The day before we left for Cooma unfortunately saw the first snowfall of the season in the Snowy Mountains. Anyway we set off and arrived in Cooma on Mother's Day, early May in Australia.

Normally the ascent is a very easy two-hour walk but because of the snow and weather conditions it became more difficult as the walk went on and the closer we got to the summit.

We left my wife and daughters in a skier's hut and the two of us made for the final ascent, however, conditions became so treacherous underfoot with ice and the mist so thick that we had to abandon the attempt. We dug a hole and left the peace Message there. Bert's comment was 'we would have made it

OK with crampons.'

DB

Perhaps the most significant outcome of Bert's climbing, and the building of the Peace Cairn on Ben Nevis was:

Bert's visit to Japan

'Continuing his story of the Cross and the Peace Cairn,' writes Revd. Eric Challoner, 'Bert told how the Dudley and Fort William Groups had sent two tablets inscribed with messages of peace to Japan, to be put in the Hiroshima Peace garden. He then told us had been invited to go to Japan, as a guest of the Japanese government. He visited Hiroshima, and was able to see some of the survivors, the blind, the deaf, and hear first hand accounts of terrible suffering still being felt. He saw the gruesome statistics telling how on that fateful day in August 1945 just one bomb floated down from the sky over the centre of the city of 400,000 people, and had exploded killing and maiming for life more than half the population. There were tears in his eyes as he recalled some of the things that he heard and saw.

Nearly all the fire stations were destroyed. Forty of their hospitals were destroyed, leaving just three.

Two hundred and seventy doctors and one thousand six hundred and forty five of their nurses were killed in a moment of time.

'Those who died were the lucky ones' said Bert. 'Those who were maimed, and blinded, and still suffering the terrible consequences of radiation, children who had lost all their relatives, and parents who had lost their children, are the ones we should feel for most.'

He went on to say 'Yet from this very city came a message of peace and reconciliation and good will'.

I'm glad that I was able to record Bert's conversation with me, and as I have written this piece I've listened again to his voice, and include now his closing words-I wish that you could hear them for yourself.

"Whenever I climb to our Peace Cairn, I think of the millions of youth who were slaughtered in two world wars, and I imagine them saying to me 'surely there's a better way to settle the disputes than by destroying the lives of some of the most promising young people in the world. Try to settle things by peaceful means'"

He continued, "I feel that this is one of the jobs that our class has been called to do, and I feel that God has given us the Hiroshima Cross to help us to do it. So, whoever hears this tape, I do pray that you will decide to dedicate your life to Christian service of love, reconciliation, and peace."

A truly remarkable man, and I am so thankful that I went to speak to him (at the Methodist Conference) and how that conversation opened a door to a truly mountain top experience.'

EC

Some general tributes to him

'The power of prayer, a lesson to us all'

Bert was revered by all who came in contact with him. Of all his unique qualities he was foremost a man of the people. No matter how busy he was he always had time for people. No focus groups, E-mails or faxes for Bert. It was person- to -person contact. On meeting him, he always made you feel the most important person in the world. Everybody who met him, couldn't help being moved by him. In Bert, Dudley had it's own 'modem day saint'! It was his eccentric charm, which made him so popular with people. Here was truly a man of God.

Bert led a very monastic life. Everything he did was in God's name, and although he had his disappointments, he always bounced back. How did he do it? Because of one thing. The power of prayer. A lesson to us all.

Colour, class and creed meant nothing to Bert. Whether he was talking to the chief of the Clan Cameron or a humble newspaper vendor. Class meant nothing. Everybody was equal. Walking down Dudley High Street with him was quite an experience. He seemed to know everybody.

His contribution to Vicar Street was enormous. The work he did putting Dudley and Fort William on the map was immense. A freeman of both boroughs, Dudley owes so such to Bert.

In religious circles it's very easy to become very serious about theology, but Bert was a man with a great sense of humour and was always planning for the future. Best reflected in the Class mottoes "the best is yet to be" and "forward ever forward". Even in his latter days, with failing health, he was planning for the millennium. Sadly, a feat he never quite made.

Who else would send peace messages to Mount Everest, the South Pole and yes even the moon. Not forgetting the peace bottle cast adrift in mid Atlantic from the Queen Elizabeth liner. Where else but Vicar Street would you have two harvest festivals, and who could forget those walks to Coventry and night climbs up Mount Snowdon. Yes Bert always had a sense of adventure.

Let's not forget his sterling work as Dudley's first probation officer; an office he held in the town for over thirty years. All his charges were grateful for the help he gave them. They all spoke highly of him.

He could quite easily have chosen to live in a leafy country village ministering to the rich and well heeled. But that was not the life for Bert. He chose to help the petty thief, the alcoholic and those who were socially disadvantaged.

Having watched him at close quarters he had the knack of getting anybody, including complete strangers, to do anything he asked of them. He was the greatest salesman I ever met. A salesman for the Lord. Above all else he was the good shepherd shepherding his flock into church. If you didn't make it one Sunday for whatever reason, he'd say, "we missed you last Sunday."

In his own small way he probably did more for world peace than any Nobel Peace Prize winner. An MBE, winner of the world Methodist peace prize and world Rotary Club prize medal winner. Material Possessions meant nothing to him. Those who saw his front room knew his life's work was dedicated to his love of Jesus Christ.

The pinnacle of his year's work at the Bible Class would be the annual Pilgrimage to Fort William, the climb up the Ben and the laying of a poppy wreath on his beloved peace cairn on the summit. All of course culminating in his appeal for young men to step forward and give their hearts to God.

Who said the secret of long life was good, wholesome nutritious food. Those who visited 16, Selbourne Road could see Bert lived on cakes and biscuits and never cooked a meal in his life. Yet he was so physically strong, members of the party climbing the Ben couldn't keep up with him, even though he was well into his sixties at the time I first climbed with him. How fitting he should be buried in the shadow of Ben Nevis.

A gentleman with old-fashioned charm, the Bible Class reflected his charisma. Who can forget those never ending votes of thanks at the class? That in itself reflected Bert's personality. He was so grateful when people did something for him. Thank God for Bert Bissell.

Peter Walker

His single-mindedness

I have read and listened to many tributes to Bert since he died as well as during his lifetime and these seem to be the most commonly held remembrances—

Bert's single-minded determination to pursue courses of action seemingly hopeless to others, in constant belief that prayer and persistence would finally lead to fulfilment.

His acceptance of all people, regardless of class, colour, caste or background, accepted through faith into God's family where redemption was not only possible, but guaranteed.

His steadfast encouragement which always left people feeling good about themselves and valued, not just at the time of meeting, but long afterwards, and often for a lifetime.

Countless people could give moving testimony to their contacts with Bert and the influence his living faith has had on their lives. I can tell only of my own experiences, which you can multiply a thousand times over, and then a thousand times again, as Bert's message of peace has been carried around the world and continues to speak from mountain tops to the young and adventurous of all nations.

I came to Dudley as a teacher of Religious Studies in 1986, and one of the senior members of staff recommended that I invite Bert into the school to speak to the pupils. Somewhat wary of inviting an eighty-four-year old to speak to pupils of fourteen, I sought the advice of some of my more knowledgeable colleagues in the woodwork room tea club, who said I would not be disappointed.

Bert Bissell came and entranced the children and entranced me. He was clearly an extraordinary character and made several visits to the school while I was there.

I can remember taking carloads of children to sit with him in his famous living room, just to take in the extraordinary collection of memorabilia which he had assembled during his remarkable lifetime, and to listen to what he had to say. Of course the kettle would go on and tea and biscuits, and often a bowl of strawberries would appear!

My son, James, was christened at Vicar Street three years later and now, at the tender age of nine, is one of the youngest members of the Vicar Street Bible Class.

In 1988 1 was involved in a testing 400-mile relay run from Dudley to Fort William to celebrate Bert's I 100th ascent of Ben Nevis. Bert was there to greet us on our arrival in Fort William and all the boys and girls who completed the relay joined the party to climb the Ben for a mountain top service in mist and rain on the following day.

It is hard to conceive of anyone of that age, who could retain such a driving, active interest in life as Bert did. Indeed, his climb was sponsored to support Methodist Homes for the Aged, most of the beneficiaries being twenty years his junior!

In the last couple of years I have witnessed some holy and spiritual occasions at Vicar Street which will never be forgotten.

I can remember arriving on one Sunday afternoon to see an old member of the class who had been in hospital for months, battling against illness. He arrived outside the church with his doctor, (a Muslim), a great, soft spoken bear of a man who picked up his patient and carried him across the road to the church door. Bert, at the age of ninety-four, was running across the road behind them carrying his friend's Zimmer frame!

Barely well enough to speak, Bert insisted that our brother should do so. Watched by his doctor, he recited his beloved 23rd Psalm, 'The Lord is my Shepherd'. He spoke of each verse and how it had sustained him, and he spoke of old times to his friends on what was his last visit to the class.

The doctor declined an invitation from Bert to give an address but went from the platform where he sat as a guest of honour and stood with his hand firmly grasping the shoulder of his patient - declared him his friend, and expressed as a Muslim how privileged he felt to be in such a Holy place.

Now that was a moment of purity - the essence of Bert's ministry, and an embodiment of the character of the Vicar Street Bible Class.

Bert was a fiercely independent man, and it took a great deal of effort from many of us to persuade him to accept a greater measure of help at his home in Selborne Road. Shortly after we succeeded, he had his fall, and as he moved from Russell's Hall to Corbett, to Nethercrest Nursing Home, it was clear to all of us he was reaching the end of his life.

Many praises have been given to Bert, but none so great as the praise and encouragement he gave to others.

Councillor Richard Burt, 24th November 1998

The Revd Dr. John Sampson, Chairman of the Wolverhampton and Shrewsbury District of the Methodist Church speaking at the Thanksgiving Service for Bert.

This afternoon we have listened to a kaleidoscopic picture of an extraordinary man. His life touched innumerable people in a wide variety of ways. Now at the end of this afternoon, we ask, what held together the pattern of his life? The answer is, clearly, his Christian commitment as mediated through the Methodist tradition. He was the son of a Methodist minister and imbibed its faith and ethos from his earliest days.

Recently Methodists have been sharing in the annual Covenant service using the words which he will often have done:

'I am no longer my own but yours, put me to what you will, rank me with whom you will

Put me to doing, put me to suffering; let me be employed for you or laid aside for you,

Exalted for you or brought low for you.

Let me be full, let me be empty. Let me have all things, let me have nothing. I freely and wholeheartedly yield all things to you pleasure and disposal.'

This was at the very heart of Bert's spirituality.

He knew also that in the rule for Methodist preachers, John Wesley had told his assistants to go 'not only to those who need you but to those who need you most' and he sought to deal with those who were the most disadvantaged in our society, to reach the excluded and to embrace them within the welcome of the Christian Gospel.

And moreover, he believed, that in accordance with his tradition God would not only save people but he would save them to the uttermost. He believed that it was possible that God would bring people to a level of maturity that they never imagined that they would achieve and that they could become the kind of beings whom God desired them to be. So his message, even with those in the most difficult circumstances, was always full of hope.

Today, we give thanks for a Christian gentleman. It is impossible to estimate the worth of a totally dedicated life, but this life was such a one. Thanks be to God for him. May he rest in peace.

John T.W. Sampson

Bert, the 'Good Friend'

The following tribute from Titus Gordon is a reminder of the way in which Bert made arrivals from the West Indies welcome to the Class.

'I arrived in Britain in early 1960. A young man of 20 years of age. No friends socially.

My nuclear family in this country was not very well associated with my extended family back in Jamaica. I soon started to make friends. I met a dear friend who introduced me to Mr. Bissell at his Fireside meeting on a Friday night.

I did not like the Fireside meeting very much. However, I joined in. There we would sing a hymn and read from the Bible. Then Mr. Bissell would give an address. At the end of the meeting, he said that he was- pleased to see me and he was looking forward to seeing me the following Friday at 8pm. I did not want to get back to his Fireside because (the weather) was cold and damp, but he took my name and my address. In those days I was living in lodgings. During the week Mr. Bissell visited me and said that he was looking forward to seeing me on the Friday evening, and so as not to disappoint him I attended. And he asked me to be the Chairman at the Class on Sunday afternoon. I did not know what to do because I had never been a chairman before, but I accepted. I was shaking like a leaf at being Chairman.

Since then I have become a loyal member and friend of Mr. Bissell and his Bible Class. I have had the privilege of representing his Bible Class at other organisations in Dudley, including the CRC (now Racial Equality Committee) and 'Dudley One World'. Through Vicar St. Methodist Men's Class I have been a member of Dudley One World Week which seeks to promote racial harmony and educate everyone, regardless of race, colour or creed, in sharing this beautiful world of which we are all part.

I have been very saddened by the passing away of Mr. Bissell from this side of consciousness. I am sure he has joined the other saints and prophets who have gone before us. I am sure that on this plane Mr. Bissell will never be replaced or be forgotten. He will be remembered throughout the world for his dedicated work for world peace.

May the Divine Essence of the Cosmic Being ever remain with Mr. Bissell. May he rest in peace until his Master comes.

Titus

'Wouldn't take 'No' for an answer'

One of my memories of Bert was the day myself, Bert, my brother Peter and Terry Flavell went to London to meet Sir Douglas Bader. What a day that was.

Bert wanted to thank Sir Douglas Bader for a letter he had sent to someone in Dudley who had lost his legs.

Terry Flavell took us to New St. Station in Birmingham in his little Morris Minor. Terry wasn't the best driver in the world but we got there safely. We caught the train to London, then a Taxi to Sir Douglas' home 'in a quiet "mews" in London. Douglas wasn't at home but at work in the Civil Aviation building in the heart of London. Back in the taxis.

No appointment was made and Sir Douglas wouldn't see us. Bert pointed out we had come a long way and would wait to see him. Eventually he gave in and we shuffled into his office. Only to be asked by Sir Douglas why weren't we all at work? Bert tried to get him to come to the Bible Class to no avail.

After a photograph and handshakes we left. Still it proved who was the most stubborn, Bert or one of our country's bravest Second World War heroes.

A day never to be forgotten.

Steve Walker

'Youth is a relative term'

There are still those who welcome us at the class as 'young men' We might even be retired ourselves; 'it all depends by what you mean by old!'

'On the 21st of June 1990 writes Doug Timmis, a group of us from our Church were invited to lead the Sunday afternoon Young Men's Bible Class at Vicar Street Methodist Church, and then we had tea with Bert and his friends.

Since then, some of us have often joked together, for Bert would refer to those 'Wonderful Young People at Balsall Common', and by young he meant the likes of John Alldrett (– the not so young).

Bert wrote to me 'thanking God for introducing him to the people of our Church' on that Sunday morning in November 1991. It was a special day for us, and I think it was because his presence aroused something within us.

We thank God for his life, friendship and example.

DT

16 Selbourne Road - *A house never forgotten*

'I also recall being invited by Bert to visit him at his home in Dudley when he had the opportunity of showing me so many items of memorabilia which he had collected from various parts of the world in his work for peace. I was asked to remain for tea and in his humble way Bert Bissell looked after me like royalty. We sat in the front room of his home with the finest of china, the old fashioned tea pot and Bert served bread and butter, pineapple and carnation cream. It was at this meeting that I learned that over the years Bert had maintained a diary which he completed on a daily basis before prayers on retiring to bed. Bert also prayed every morning.

Roger Baguley, Former Chief Constable of Dudley

'Stories I heard at my father's knee'

'My earliest memories of Bert Bissell,' writes Viv Turner, 'are as a small child standing at my father's knee and listening to stories of how The Vicar Street Young Men's Bible Class was formed and how my father had been invited to join at the age of sixteen in 1926. He told me of Bert's goodness and how he instinctively knew when people needed his help and how he was always available for them. My father told me how he used to rely on Bert and that he was guided by him, particularly during his teenage years.

As well as my father, my husband and son are also members of The Bible Class and over the years it has been with pride that I have seen these three generations going in unity to Bert's Class week by week. Both my husband and son have taken an active part in the class activities and I know that this has given them much satisfaction.

As an adult I have known Bert as a true friend for many years. He has always been there when I needed him and there have been many times when I have been fearful and in distress when we have talked and he has prayed with me and I have become calm and able to face up to life's adversities. I know that his guiding hand has helped me through the most difficult times that I have had to face.

When my father and my husband have been ill in hospital I knew that I could depend upon Bert to be one of their first visitors. I have been in the hospital ward and have felt uplifted to see his slight figure walking in his own inimitable way towards us, his face wreathed in smiles and always with his offering of a bar of chocolate. Bert always looked after his flock.

Memories can never be erased from our minds but I think it is good to have something tangible to hold on to after the loss of a dear one. We have our own personal photographs taken of Bert when we visited each other and I am glad that I paid tribute to him in both of my books, the words of which he said pleased him well. There was a twinkle in Bert's eye as he sat in front of the mural on the wall in his rear sitting room with Ben Nevis immediately behind him. I think we succeeded in giving the impression that Bert was in his beloved Scotland. Bert had a great sense of humour.

Bert had many anecdotes. He told us that on one occasion he was asked to procure no less than three billiard tables for the benefit of the boys of an approved school. With the benefit of prayer and his formidable powers of determination and persuasion Bert managed to find all three tables and to arrange for them to be delivered. Bert would describe how as a young man he relinquished his livelihood in Coventry to come to Dudley where he established his Bible Class. The numbers in the class grew, through this he was able to help those who were in trouble in the juvenile court. The expertise he thus acquired led to his appointment later to the position of Probation Officer for Dudley, which he conducted from the shed at the side of his home in Selbourne Road. Bert would also of course describe his mountaineering adventures and I recall his description of his dangerous climb with one of his brothers in Switzerland when he feared for his life.

The greatest tribute that we can pay Bert is to continue The Bible Class just as he would have wished and I hope erect a monument in memory of this wonderful man of Dudley who gave so much to all of us and who will be sadly missed and who is irreplaceable. However, new younger members of the Class will be needed as many of the former 'Young Men' of the class are no longer young.

We consider ourselves in our family most privileged to have known Bert. Sadly my father died last year and it was a comfort to me to have Bert present at my father's funeral and to share time together in my home afterwards. I could not have known that in a few short months I would be attending Bert's own funeral.'

VT

A few brief tributes passed on to us from the Dudley Express and Star, under the main newspaper headline:

'Mountain of Peace' man Bert dies, 96'

Colin Bissell – Nephew –(only relative living in the Black Country) 'He was a kind and considerate man who had a lot of time and compassion for everyone. We were close and will miss him a great deal.'

Colin Dunn – a friend of 50 years and vice-president of the Worcestershire Boy's Brigade Battalion. 'He was a wonderful man. Even as a younger person he had an ability to make you feel the most important person that he had met that day.'

Viv. Asting, Dudley Council's Chief executive. 'One of the town's outstanding sons.' His compassion, charity work and commitment to world peace were and will be an inspiration to everyone.'

Dudley's Mayor, Councillor Ken Finch said 'I was so sad to hear that one of Dudley's outstanding sons had passed away.

Bert Bissell was a great influence for the good in the borough. His compassion, charity work and commitment to world peace, and will continue to be, an inspiration to everyone... Known and loved by many in the borough, Bert is sadly missed and the world is poorer for his passing.'

-and The Bishop of Dudley

The Rt. Revd. Dr Rupert W.N. Hoare wrote:

'I have a huge admiration for Bert, as so many of us do. I suppose I did not know him particularly well, but I have visited him at home, and I preached at his invitation to the Bible Class at Vicar Street each year since I have been here.

I also went to Ben Nevis on the 50th Anniversary of the end of the war in Japan and well remember Bert at the bottom of the mountain, saying goodbye to us all as we set off, and greeting us as we returned. From those simple encounters, I got a clear view of his Gospel priorities, great humanity, and tremendous affirmation of all those that he came into contact with. Also of course, his commitment to peace across the world was palpable and so strong, as we celebrated together that August afternoon the worship of God on the top of Ben Nevis with Bert himself having to stay at the bottom, and doubtless longing to have been up at the top!

I am so glad I got to know him at least a little, towards the end of his life. His influence on so many people in Dudley and the whole area has been and will remain profound without any doubt.

Rupert Dudley

The Bert Bissell Memorial Stone at the Town Hall, Dudley. Left to right - back: The Provost of Fort William, Revd. Inderjit Bhogal (Chairman of the Methodist Conference, 2001), Andrew Sparke (Chief Executive of Dudley); front: Councillor Goerge Davies (The Mayor of Dudley)

Things never forgotten

This next section includes many short extracts from letters which remind us again of Bert's great capacity for making friendships, being involved in opening unexpected doors, and his great adaptability.

'Ever widening circles of friendship'

Louie and Jim Beddall, life time supporters of the Class, write.

'A few years ago I read an article in a Sunday newspaper about who owns the top part of Ben Nevis. I gave the cutting to Jim and he took it to the Bible class for Bert. The following day Bert traced these people to their home at Stratford on Avon. He told them all about the Cairn on the top of the Ben, the friendship that has grown from the Bible Class to many parts of the world, and the many ways our Christian Belief and our Heavenly Father have helped this to happen.

They were very impressed and thought it was a wonderful story. They are very nice people who take a leading part in their own Church activities. They invited Bert, Jim and myself to their home to tea. Bert was so delighted – another link had been forged with his beloved Ben Nevis and Fort William, and he invited the gentleman to speak at our Bible Class on two separate occasions.'

L&JB

'It led to Myanmar (Burma)'

The Revd. Ivan Homer, himself a native of the Black Country, recalls the time he was in training for the Methodist Ministry at Headingley.

'One Sunday I went along to the Bible Class. The speaker was the Revd. Edgar Nicholson, a missionary on furlough from Burma, the first missionary on active service in that country. Bert introduced me to him after the service. Little did I know at that time that immediately following my training in college, I would serve as a missionary myself in Burma for ten years. It was there too that I met my wife Ruth, who also involved in missionary work there.'

Ivan also recalls how he had seen Bert at various times in his ministry when he 'would turn up at events like Synods and Conference with three or four young people in tow' *This was in the days before the church insisted that conferences should have a proper representation of younger people.*

IH

'Mr. Putty Fingers'

Frank Nicklin remembered Bert visiting the home of his parents 58 years ago when his dad died and he himself was seven years old. 'He came to offer his help in any way, he did in many ways. I myself used to call him "Mr. Putty fingers" because he always shook one's hand on arrival. It proves one thing - *Cold hand and surely a warm heart.* God bless you Bert.

FN

His favourite team remembered him

Ian Townsend visited his mother in the Corbett hospital at the same time that Bert was there. Hearing that Bert was a football supporter they talked football together. Ian persuaded Coventry City to send Bert a 'get well' card which had pride of place on Bert's bedside locker. In true Black Country terms *"A Bostin bloke."*

IT

Pleasant, kind and humble

Mrs. P. Cherrington. 'Mr. Bissell was indeed a wonderful Godly person for

This was a favourite picture of Bert's that hung in his sitting room. (By courtesy of Dudley Archives)

whom Dudley and the Methodist Circuit can be very proud and privileged to have known. He was always pleasant, kind and humble. I certainly felt blessed by knowing him and reading 'God's Mountaineer.'

PC

'He shared our tragedy'

On March 6th 1997 our son Richard fell over the 1000 foot Orion face of Ben Nevis while ice climbing. He died as a result of his injuries. Mr. Bissell came to see us to offer his condolences, and attended our son's funeral at the local Catholic Church. A week later he visited us and asked if he could arrange a memorial service at Vicar Street Methodist Church. As the parents of Richard we felt highly honoured by this gesture.

The service was made very moving and special to us by the welcome of the congregation and the many efforts Mr. Bissell had put in to make it so. During the memorial service Mr. Bissell presented us with a beautiful Bible on behalf of the Class. Many months later he again came to spend some time with us to see how we were coping with our sad loss. A more considerate, kind and religious man we have yet to meet. May God bless him and keep him in his care...

Anne and Leonard Simcox.

The St. Stephen's Walkers

Pat Walton the Church Council Secretary of St. Stephen's Methodist Church, Cannock, sends the following extract from the Annual Church Meeting minutes of her church.

'It is ten years this summer since our Walkers' Group was formed. I wonder how many people will remember the visit of that well-known 'Black Country Walker', Bert Bissell, to our Church Home Missions Meeting in 1984 when he spoke to us about his experience of climbing mountains – for it was that visit that inspired US to climb mountains and get walking!

Even though our ages have increased by some fourteen years since we started, we all get together for our Annual Dinner early in the year, and while all the walkers do not belong to St. Stephen's some members coming from as far afield as Wolverhampton, Stafford and Cannock Wood – such is the attraction of this friendly group – support is given to the Church in many ways, including the raising of funds for our current 'Building Bridges in the Community' project.

We are thankful to Bert Bissell, whose message at our Home Missions Meeting gave us the incentive to take up this healthy outdoor pursuit.'

PW

Class Truants

'My brother Peter and I,' writes Bob Nicholls, 'were members of Vicar Street Young Men's' Bible Class round about 1950. I would be fifteen and

Peter thirteen. We used to go regularly to the class, twice some Sundays.

'We went to Fort William and climbed Ben Nevis with Bert. The itinerary schedule was sealed in a bottle and placed in the Cairn. So our names are still close to Bert. We slept on the floor in Church Halls and school halls in Fort William and Inverness and really enjoyed it.

'As we got older and interest in the class waned – I think it changed to girls and snooker! We started missing classes. Bert would come to our house, on his bike to ask where we were. Rather than face him with excuses, we would run down the garden, climb over the wall and be off... I remember telling him it was too far to walk, so he offered to send a taxi for us. We never took him up on this offer, but still have fond memories of Bert and all he did to help anyone he came across.'

BN

How did he do it?

Derek Bissell makes a further contribution to this anthology.

In August 1998 I went over to Dudley to see Bert, he was in the Corbett Hospital at the time. He gave me the OK to go to 16 Selbourne Road and sort through the many papers and do some culling. As I went through the volumes of information stretching back decades I became more and more amazed at the scope and endeavour of his life and the enormity of his faith and conviction.

After leaving Selbourne Road I would then go to the hospital and spend an hour with him. During one visit I said to him:

"Bert, just how did you do it all?"

He replied very simply and with emotion, *"With Divine assistance!"*

DB

Tributes from other Class members - past and present

Whether we still live in the Dudley area or not we are all still considered Class Members. The following contributions are from a mixture of us in both categories.

A week before Bert died, Pauline and I went to see him. We arrived shortly after Alastair Bissell, his great nephew, who was still there with him. He was obviously very pleased to see us all. His deafness made it very hard to have any real conversation with him, but one thing he said was this. *'It is of God, God is in this.'*

I found myself puzzled. It might have been his illness that made him say these words, and Bert was always looking in every situation to see where God was at work in what was going on, but I felt there might well be another explanation. Alastair and I hardly knew each other because we had been members of the class in different stages of its history. We belonged to different generations. Here perhaps, at Bert's bedside was an opportunity for us to recognise the common bond of faith and experience in a faith that we had come to know so much about, through Bert.

My weekly attendance at the class had been while Bert was still busily working as a probation officer in Dudley.

As with many other members of the class however, the Institute at the rear of the Church, now derelict, was where our earlier ventures in faith began. There, many of us made our first commitment to Christ. The experiential and intellectual nurture that we received there from Bert, every Monday and Friday evening was phenomenal. Very significantly, to many of us, the Institute was originally built as a stable. It reminded us of another stable 'where it all began.'

The Sunday afternoon Bible Class however was the mainstay of our worship -but wherever those of us who felt a call to the ordained ministry went later in life, there was always Bert's prayerful support at 'home base' and from time to time he sent us his words of encouragement wherever we were. This has been such a source of help and strength to those of us in the ministry over the years.

On the day of Bert's funeral at Vicar Street, Inderjit told us that Bert was already retired before he even knew him. It was also true for the 'ministry formation' period of Alastair Bissell, and Albert Gayle who were also taking part in the service.

In the later stages of his life Bert carried his work with continued diligence and enthusiasm, continually finding new avenues, especially in what I like to call 'The Ministry of the Third Age,' which included encouraging older people

Stained glass window at Vicar Street representing: The Nativity, The Class, The World, The Cairn on Ben Nevis and The Dove symbolising Peace and Goodwill.

to fulfil active roles in the community as well as younger people. Many of the 'Gentleman Songsters' for instance who were in this age group greatly appreciated the encouragement that he gave.

The class over its history has given a tremendous number of young men encouragement to reach out towards their potential for God. Let us never forget however, Bert was a tremendous example and help to older people too.

'Challenge' to him was for *the whole* of life. Whatever stage of life he was in, he had that kind of spirituality which saw opportunities everywhere and God speaking through every kind of situation. It is of God. God is in this.' Immediately he would start to explore how this was to be worked out.

The challenge of Bert's life will continue to inspire so many of us well into the next millennium. We thank God for his life.'

DM

'Prayer knows no racial barriers'

'As I sit down to write this,' says The Revd. Albert Gayle, 'I am thinking about the recent report of the Stephen Lawrence inquiry. I am thinking about phrases like 'pernicious and institutionalised racism'. But I am also aware of the young men who are alleged to have killed Stephen Lawrence. Who and what is responsible for the condition we name racism? Where do innocent looking children get their ideas of racism from? Parents? Teachers? Is it an innate condition? Do we absorb these characteristics from the social, economic and political conditions in which we live? We may never agree on the source of racism since it is multifaceted, but who will rescue us?

I can't help but contrast all that with someone who could have exhibited those traits in his life, but instead lived an exemplary life. For a man of his generation, Bert Bissell has shown a remarkable life of holiness to young and old, black and white. Never, in all the years that I have known him, has he ever given a hint that the colour of someone's skin was a challenge to him. I am not surprised that his Bible Class at Vicar Street in Dudley flourished with people from different cultures and traditions. He was never embarrassed or ashamed to be associated with people on the margins. In truth, he relished it, not only locally but nationally and internationally.

What was his secret? I believe that his secret was to be found in prayer. He prayed for those in his pastoral care.

He was such an unassuming, sensitive and gentleman. One of the outstanding things about Bert was his ability to draw out the hidden potential in a person. He has been doing that for a long time.

I remember that when I was a teenager in Dudley he used to come to my home in North Street every Saturday morning to encourage me to come to the Bible Class on the Sunday afternoon. I knew when he would be coming and I am afraid that sometimes I tried to avoid him. On one occasion when there was snow on the ground I stayed in because I thought he was unlikely to come in such bad weather. I was proved wrong when he came as usual. His determination and courage was such that it was useless trying to hide. He had won me for Christ without my knowing it at the time. Bert must have seen the potential in me or he would have given up on me long ago.

As a result of his persistence I went to the Bible Class and later he encouraged me to go to Cliff College and then to become a candidate for the Methodist ministry. Up until his death he continued to give prayerful support, love and encouragement.

It was very appropriate that on the same day that I was ordained at the Methodist Conference in Portsmouth in 1987, Bert received the Methodist Peace Prize. It was a very moving experience to sit on the platform as an ordinand and hear the tributes to the person who had played such a vital part in leading me to that point.

Bert was an example of the way God works quietly and in places where we least expect him through the faith and love of his people. Through him we have been challenged to believe in the God who transcends all barriers. We have been challenged to find our security through a relationship of prayer.

It is by following the example of Bert and others like him who point us to Christ, that we can be rescued from the sin of racism.'

Albert Gayle

..and 'Hopes for a Spiritual Classic'

I have somewhere a photograph of Bert standing outside Buckingham

The Sunday School Staff of Vicar Street Methodist Church. 1st May 1950. Left to right - back: Alan Wedge, John Nott, Tony Wesson, Iris Cope, Freda Taylor, R.Baker, Ernest Bissell, A Fisher, Jim Bradley, Jean Chapple, Ray Bissell. Louie Onions, Cyril Edwards(secretary) Jack Shuker (Superintendent) Peggy Onions, A Vanes; front: Bill Parkes, David Monkton.

Palace taken after the ceremony to receive his MBE. The one aspect of this that has always remained in my memory is that shortly after he had received it I congratulated him on this achievement, to which he replied that 'it was nothing compared with the honour of being called by God into the service of Jesus Christ.' This comment was typical of Bert and I think it is a perfect indication of the kind of person he was.

Also I note that there is no mention of the fact that he kept a detailed diary - in the time I knew him best (in the 40's he kept a page-a-day desk diary and each page was filled with small neat hand writing. I never read any of the comments of course - I don't think anyone was allowed to - but he told me that he kept a record of all that happened in the Class and especially of experiences and the thoughts arising from these.

My hope is' writes the Revd. Allan Stanton 'that at an appropriate time some suitable person might edit them. They would no doubt prove to be a Spiritual Classic.'

AS

It started at the Fire Station

The following is a tribute made to Bert by The Revd. Ken Collins at the Wolverhampton and Shrewsbury Synod in September 1995.

'I have known Bert now for over 45 years. We actually met at Dudley Fire station where I had been taken by a school friend to join in a visit arranged by Bert.

As a former member of the Bible Class and as one who candidated for the Ministry from Vicar Street I have been asked by the Chairman to perform "Mission Impossible." That is, in a few minutes to pay tribute to a multigifted, multifaceted man who has so many achievements to his name. I hope you will forgive the fact that I am going to couch what I have to say in personal terms but then ask you to go on to multiply what is said many times over.

Pastoral Care: Bert is supremely effective in pastoral care. He has a remarkable record of visitation of class members. Mind you, there were times when it could have some disadvantages. A neighbour once met my mother in Dudley Market Place, you know, that centre of the weekly shop before they opened Merry Hill. She asked my mother what sort of trouble my brother and I were in as she had seen the Probation Officer visiting our house regularly.

Probation Officer. You see Bert was *the* Probation Officer, indeed from the earliest days he *was* the probation service in Dudley and was responsible for the development of that service in the Dudley area. For me, Bert epitomised the phrase in earlier childcare legislation which talked about 'befriending' young people. Indeed it was his example upon which I based my own approach to social work as I engaged in seeking to meet the needs of young people and families.

Walker and Mountaineer. This has been a supreme aspect of Bert's life and many people have benefited from the pilgrimages to the top of the Ben. I, myself will never forget the tremendous experience of watching the dawn rise from the top of Ben Nevis and the effect of that experience on my life. Or the occasion when on the way up the mountain Bert came to me and said, "Ken, you will conduct the service round the cairn". Since that time I have never been able to live down the label of 'high church!'

Man of Peace. Moving out from the Cairn on Ben Nevis, links have been developed both on a national and international scale as Bert has applied a large proportion of his life to exploring ways of linking people. We must not forget that this has also led to civic honours with Bert being made a Freeman of the Borough. Incidentally, Bert, there is something that I have always wanted to know and perhaps you will tell me afterwards – when you are made a Freeman, can you actually go everywhere free of charge?

Bridge Builder. Through the seventy years of the Class Bert has always made sure of building bridges between people, and has played a special part in ensuring that the approach has been multiracial... In fact Bert has been a true bridge builder and if the Roman Catholic Church can have a pontiff, Mr. Chairman, why should not the Methodist Church also have its own pontiff?

Bert, on behalf of all of here at Synod, may I wish you many more years of building bridges and peace making. God bless you.

Ken Collins

Bert – the Family Man

The Revd. Alastair Bissell was one of the speakers at the Civic Memorial Service held at the Dudley Town Hall early in the January of 1999. This was the theme of his message.

'To try and condense a life in a few short moments is a difficult scenario in itself. When you come to the life of Bert Bissell, such a task is well nigh impossible. Each of you will have your own special and fond memories of this man of God... As a member of his family, I saw another side to Bert that perhaps only some saw. He was very much a family man, who cared deeply for his own flesh and blood.

At Selbourne Road where, along with my father Don, and brother Martin, and the rest of the clan, Bert played host.

You were treated like royalty. Out came the chocolate biscuits, freshly baked bread, cream cakes. There was even a double helping of trifle if Coventry had won.

We would often sit down for the hour following the class, holding discussions upon topical events. The front room especially resembled a gallery of mementoes form all over the world, which was typical of his capacity to look outwards.

Even at a young age, one was taken with this deeply caring and genuine man who had the capacity to take an active interest in all that you were doing – be it at home, work, or school. You were made to feel special and important.

Over subsequent years 16 Selbourne Road became not just for the family, a place of pilgrimage, but to all who knocked on the famous front door. For they too would always be welcomed. Often Bert would contemplate with them where they were on their spiritual journey.

I recall one of the first ever times I was asked to chair the class, and we all know to refuse was never an option.

Bert, as we know, liked to give instructions, and firmly expected them to be carried out. He gave the speakers about twenty minutes and no more.

A certain preacher liked the sound of his own voice, so much so, that over thirty five minutes had elapsed when members of the class were becoming restless. Bert sensed this, and offered words of encouragement 'Amen' he said on more than one occasion. Yet the minister failed to take the hint: that was until I heard Bert turn to him and whisper, "Is it still Sunday?"

He promptly sat down and had to wait a while for his next invitation.

Bert saw humour as part of his ministry. He firmly believed that no one was beyond redemption, even when others were giving up as a lost cause, he felt that the kingdom of God welcomed all, not matter what anyone's past history was. A new start with Christ was always a distinct possibility.

There's no doubt that during his 96 years of service, Bert's contribution has been felt not only by his family, but all over the world. In many ways, he firmly believed that the world was his family.

Let me close this tribute by offering this illustration.

I well remember some members of the class travelling down to the capital city, where Bert had an appointment at the Japanese Embassy. After the business was concluded, we went on a visit to various landmarks, this included the famous St. Paul's Cathedral. My uncle took us to the crypt where the tombs of the great and famous are laid to rest, including that of Sir Christopher Wren, the Architect of St. Paul's.

Above this tomb were the words, 'Reader, if you seek a monument then look about yourself.' In other words, don't necessarily look over your shoulder to see what others can achieve, instead look to yourself, and discover what God can achieve in your life.

The life of Bert Bissell is a living testimony to the work and the power of Christ. There are times when someone of Bert's vision is raised to do a profound work for the Kingdom.

We have all been uniquely privileged to share in a life that has been used in remarkable ways. I finish with these inimitable words of the man of God. "Forward, ever forward.... The best is yet to be."

AB

...and finally in this chapter a word from –

Astley Blake, present leader of the Bible Class

'I first came in contact with Bert Bissell, the gentle and most friendly man in Dudley, one evening on my way from work on the 245 Bus. I sat upstairs in a seat on my own. From the Dudley Guest hospital this gentleman came and sat by me, offered his hand of friendship and we enter into conversation.

On arriving at Fisher Street, Dudley, we both get off the bus and out came one of his leaflets and the invitation to attend the Bible Class at Vicar Street.

He was so friendly and unassuming that this short conversation left an impression on me. So I try to find out more about this man. I show this leaflet to a friend of mine, Dalton Bruce, who had already fallen for the gentle, God-fearing man of Dudley. He invited me to join him on the Sunday afternoon at the class.

I was made most welcome by everyone, who was so friendly. This was after visiting other churches around the area to find a spiritual home where I would be happy to worship.

Soon I was invited to 'The Fireside' meeting on a Monday night, and then the Prayer Group meeting on Friday nights. I used to make myself late to avoid some of the tasks – of having a word in prayer, or giving a vote of thanks.

I well remember one Monday night, at the end of the meeting, Bert asked that someone might give a vote of thanks. Everyone sat still, looking at one another.

Bert seeing no attempt was being made said, "Astley – you want to say something?"

I nearly said 'no' but my heart wouldn't allow me. As we all know it was very hard to say 'no' to him. I got up and mumbled something. Out came the encouraging words "Well done, Astley."

After that I was encouraged to give a little talk at the meetings, then to be chairman at the class – things that I didn't believe I could do.

After a while, out came the invitation to study for Local Preaching. I turned him down. As you all know Bert never gave up, but he kept asking saying 'You can do it.' Eventually I accepted the challenge and I am now in training.

When he was ill I tried to visit him two or three times a week and offer my assistance. He was unable to come to his beloved Bible class, so he asked myself and Jim Brookes to look after The Class for him until he was better. The unfortunate happened, and I am left in the very fortunate position of looking after the Bible Class.

My wife Elaine and myself went to see him after telling him about the arrangements for The Class. He said to me "Astley, will you promise me that you will not give up on me?" This, I assured him, I will continue to do while God gives me the strength.

For a short period these certificates were presented to members of the class in place of badges (see page 37)

The words which come to mind are from Paul's first letter to Timothy where The Apostle says: *'To this end we toil and strive because we have our hope set on the living God, who is the saviour of all men, especially of those who believe'* (ch4 vs10)

AB

Summing up The Journey

It seems appropriate at this point to include the Tribute Given to Bert at the Funeral Service held at Vicar Street by the Revd. Inderjit Bhogal, this year's President of the Methodist Conference.

'We are all here because Bert Bissell has died. We are all here because the life and death of Bert Bissell has touched us all. We've lost someone special. May God grant peace to the man of peace.

It is thoroughly appropriate that we meet in Vicar Street Chapel, the base of Bert Bissell's life and ministry.

Bert, blessed soul that he was, died on the second of November, All Soul's Day, within All Saint's Tide, and remarkably as his funeral service is close to Armistice Day. He would have been in Fort William and up the Ben this week.

The Gospel story that comes to mind is from Luke 24, Jesus walking to Emmaus with disciples who felt they had lost a dear and special friend. He encouraged them to talk about him. 'Tell me about the things that have happened,' he said to them.

We all have a story. Our own life story, yes, but each one of us could tell dozens of marvellous stories about Bert. I am privileged to be invited to share a few now. I would encourage you to tell your stories of Bert. Tell them often. Keep his memory alive.

(It was partly as a result of this comment, and a conversation that followed the service that this book of tributes was compiled.)

Bert Bissell has been one of the most genuine human beings I have known. He has been one of *the* finest leaders of *men* I have known. His secret I believe has been that he always trusted and respected each individual. I think that all present here would individually vouch for that. Being in his company has always been an affirming and edifying experience. He had the capacity to give over time and individual attention, and the feeling that one was being listened to. And anyone always came away from a meeting with Bert Bissell feeling good about oneself, that one had worth and value. He did not make this into a crusade. This was simply his lifestyle. His inspiration and model, as he would say, " the young man of Nazareth, Jesus Christ."

Bert's home, in Selbourne Road, contains a remarkable collection of precious items. One of them is a painting he first came across in Dudley Art Gallery. He obtained a copy for himself.[4] The painting shows an old man at prayer in a chapel.

That's Bert Bissell. A man of prayer.

However else he is remembered, let him be remembered as a man of prayer. A deeply spiritual man.

Numerous stories and accolades will be spoken in reference to Bert, but let this not be lost in the midst of them all – that he prayed and that his life was seeped, soaked in prayer.

He had lists with names and organisations and issues he prayed for. He believed this was his particular calling – to pray for people. He did this – without making it, or feeling it to be a burden.

This was the heart and soul of the man. He was supported in this ministry by a small group who met with him on Friday evenings. This quiet, hidden ministry that Bert Bissell offered should not unheeded, unrecognised or undervalued. He was a deeply spiritual, holy man. Everything Bert did and achieved needs to be seen this context of prayer and spirituality:

- The Young Men's Bible Class and its midweek Fireside and Prayer meetings that he led for nearly 80 years; although the younger men and some women used to get frustrated that women couldn't be part of the class! In the light of all the interest in men's needs and responsibilities today he was ahead of his time.
- The million miles or so that he walked, and only in the last few years with professional walking boots and gear, climbing his beloved Ben Nevis with the Peace Cairn, and the highest peaks also in England, Wales and Ireland. He climbed throughout Europe, and also in Australia and South Africa. I remember when a group of us carried a tablet of stone weighing a hundredweight up the Ben in 1968!
- The walks to Coventry and Worcester, often to raise money for Dudley Town FC – a lost cause!
- The forging of international relationships, especially with Hiroshima, Japan. Bert had moved beyond the issue of forgiveness in relation to Japan, to form new bases for harmonious relationships.
- Sending peace messages to the moon, the sea, and so many mountains, with safe hands and feet of people like Chris Bonnington.
- Collecting thousands of pounds for Charities and groups like the Mountain Rescue teams, rattling tins for them in the streets, shopping arcades, and cinemas.
- Being a blood donor, he gave as many pints of blood as his age.
- All his seminal and pioneering work as a probation officer.
- Being a Local Preacher and public speaker in great demand for over 60 years.
- Taking film shows and assemblies in schools throughout the borough.
- All his work with people of different faiths and nationalities
- And even supporting Coventry City FC
- Maintaining strong links with Coventry Cathedral Chapel of Unity.

… and so much else that he somehow embraced.

All this has to be seen in the context of prayer and spirituality. Bert Bissell did not divide his living into sections of sacred and spiritual. His whole life was one great connected chain of prayer. He was a holy man. I could say of him using an Indian term, that he was a Guru - a wise, prayerful companion through all the ups and downs of life.

Holiness of the quality that shone from Bert Bissell is in short supply today. 'By their fruits you shall know' true disciples, said Jesus. All the fruits of the Spirit come together to form holiness. We saw it in Bert Bissell. It was holiness immersed in life, not detached from it. He made things of the spirit interesting, not boring. In all the challenges facing the church today, with all our confusions, conflicts and divisions, uncertainties and fears, Bert Bissell, and others like him, show us that people respond to holiness. It is the need of people of all faiths, and of people who profess no particular faith but are deeply spiritual. There is an insatiable desire, at the turn of the millennium, for qualities of holiness and saintliness.

So what are your memories of Bert? Here are a few stories from me:
- At the 50th Anniversary of the Bible Class, the start of proceedings was delayed because Bert, who usually led the Platform party out of the vestry and to their seats, was in the vestry even though everyone had taken their seat. After a minute of two of waiting I, vestry steward that afternoon, went to see where he was. I found Bert sitting in the vestry by himself – crying. I sat with him. When he was able to speak he said to me. "I'm really missing my brother Ernie. He was always such a sport." I've never repeated this story to anyone before.
- I visited Bert a few days before he died. His hearing aid was playing up, so I had to write everything I wanted to say. We had a great chat. He asked me to pray before I departed. He didn't hear a word of it, but surely God did. I stood up to go. We shook hands as usual. And Bert would not let me go. He held on fast, and wept, and wept, and wept. He was sure, I believe not,

One of Bert's walks to Coventry which included a call on David Monkton who was serving there in his first appointment as a Minister (1959)

that this would be our last meeting in this life.

I will never forget being in Fort William one year. The day arrived when we were to climb Ben Nevis. It was pouring with rain.

Bert said he would go to see what conditions were like on 'the Ben.' The rest of us were going to wait in Duncansburgh Hall. It was 8 am. At about 11 am. I suggested some of us should go and see if Bert was okay. So with me came Peter Brown and his dad and Sue Bratt. We started to walk up the Ben. It was pouring with rain. We climbed and climbed. No sign of Bert. We were getting worried. Then, at about 4000 feet we saw a figure in the distance, coming down – someone carrying an umbrella over him. It was Bert.

- Bert often told me of an occasion when he was at a farm. An international group of walkers came by and asked for drink of water. They were given water, by young Bert Bissell, from a pump. He recalled the words of Jesus; "A cup of water given in my name will have its reward."
- Bert always believed that this incident was the beginning of his hospitable attitude to people of all nations and faiths. He has developed here at the Young Men's Bible Class a genuinely multiracial community. He has shown the way to break barriers.

Tell your stories of Bert. It is sad that any story has to end with the death of this life. We would like all stories to end with 'and they all lived happily ever after.'

So, when Jesus met his two grieving friends mourning the loss of someone special, he encouraged them to about the one who had died. They poured out their story to him; they just needed a little prod. They talked, about the good things, and the bad things, and in their case a tragic untimely death of someone in the prime of life.

Jesus listened to them, and then expended on their story. He spoke of death not as the end of the story. In that particular story that The Cross, far from being the end of a dream, was paradoxically the means by which it was realised. " Was it not necessary that the Christ should suffer and (so) enter into his glory?"

Then their eyes were opened and they recognised him. The one who had died was close to them and was their companion. So death did not have the last word after all. Every human story is the story of a journey, the journey of life.

Christ is with each one of us on this journey, for some as a friend, for some as a stranger. He is so close to us that our stories, like Bert's, merge into his. And we can affirm this conviction today in the name of Bert Bissell.

When all is said and done, it is Christ's story that helps to explain and give meaning to our story. The resurrection of Christ opens all our stories to the prospect of resurrection and eternal life.

Christ is with Bert, and with us. As all our journeys, like Bert's, go on from one degree of glory to another.

Inderjit Bhogal

'We are watchers of a beacon…'

Some eighteen months after his death, at the Methodist Conference in Huddersfield, Inderjit Bhogal was inducted as President. Quite a few of us from Vicar Street were there – from every stage in the life of the class.
Somehow it was just as if Bert was around. We imagined him saying 'My werd (sic), how wonderful. We are very proud of you Inderjit.'
A friend of mine said to me, "Perhaps 'B.B.' was there!" His influence still lives on!
One of Bert's favourite hymns was written by Charles Silvester Horne, based on the hymn of the Vaudois Mountain Christians.
'For the might of thine arm we bless thee, our God, our fathers' God,
Thou hast kept thy pilgrim people by the strength of thy staff and rod;
Thou hast called us to the journey which faithless feet ne'er trod;
For the might of thine arm we bless thee, our God, our fathers' God.'
And especially the opening line in the third verse which reads,
'We are watchers of a beacon whose light must never die.'

(Hymns and Psalms no 435)

Dudley is a place that has changed tremendously during most of our life times, as have similar towns, cities and communities throughout the British Isles. The whole world has changed tremendously through the better part of a century in which Bert lived and witnessed.

Just over the road from Vicar Street there has existed now for quite a number of years, a Sikh Temple where the Locomotive Inn used to be. (The Inn was visited every Monday night by one of the older attenders at 'The Fireside' who used to amuse us teenage youths present with his 'emotionally high' recalling of religious experiences, his singing of solos from Moody and Sankey, and songs from other sources!) Just a small reminder to us that we live in a multicultural society. Very different from when many of us were born.

Bert was someone who had learnt the art of being a genuine friend to people of all faiths and outlooks – a true supporter of John Wesley's claim to be a 'friends of all and enemies of none.' One of his favourite phrases was to share the Gospel of Christ by 'ever increasing circles of friendship.' There is everything to gain and nothing to lose by looking at the model he left us to follow.

Bert was a Beacon of the last century, presenting us with a ray of light from Christ, to inspire us all into the 21st. We thank God for everything we remember about him, and that his influence will leave its mark on us all for a very long time to come.

Bibliography

[1] 'Bert Bissell, God's Mountaineer'. Methodist Publishing House 1997.
[2] 'It so happened – from plough to pulpit'. Revd. Eric Challoner. Fairway Folio (£6.99).
[3] 'Thanks to Bert.' A booklet made up of tributes from all the Ministers who entered the Methodist Ministry from Vicar Street. There are still a few copies available from David Monkton (£1.25 including p&p).

Index of contributors

Viv. Asting 57
Roger H Bagley 28
Roger Baguley 55
Louie and Jim Beddall 59
Inderjit S. Bhogal 4, 72
Alastair Bissell 68
Colin Bissell 57
Derek Bissell 48, 62
Don Bissell 6
Astley Blake 69
Peter Boxley 45
Jim Brookes 40
J. Brooks 34
Geoffrey Bruce 6
Richard Burt 53
Eric Challoner 25, 46, 49
P. Cherrington 60
George Cloke 35
Ken Collins 67
Bob Crew 41
Charlie Davenport 29
Alan Davies 8
Margaret Davies 36
Colin Dunn 57
Harold R. Eades 38
Ernest Edwards 28
Ken Finch 57
Kim Fuller 25
Albert Gayle 64
Nigel Gilson 47
Titus Gordon 54
Jeff Harbach 17
Rupert W.N. Hoare 57
Ivan Homer 27, 59

Christopher Hughes Smith
   6, 21, 44
Pat Jones 43
Karl Khan 26
Leonard W. Lloyd 28
Ron Marriott 47
Bruce Monkton 31
David Monkton 7, 64
Pauline Monkton 37
Dorothy Morgan 36
Bob Nicholls 61
Frank Nicklin 59
Freda Parkes 34
Terry Proctor 12
Stuart G. Radford 39
John Sampson 53
Anne and Leonard Simcox 61
Derek Siviter 42
Allan Stanton 66
Doug Timmis 55
Ron Towe 14
Ian Townsend 60
Mrs. Townsend 35
Viv Turner 56
Derek Vonberg 39, 43, 46
Peter Walker 51
Steve Walker 55
Pat Walton 61
Alan Wedge 7, 34
Doreen Wedge 34
Barry Weetman 6
Arthur Whale 19
Tony Willis 32